BUZAN'S BOOK OF
MENTAL
WORLD
RECORDS

Tony Buzan & Ray Keene

D&B PUBLISHING
www.dandbpublishing.com

Other Books from D & B Publishing

D & B Poker

1-904468-08-X	*How Good is your Pot-Limit Hold'em?*	Stewart Reuben
1-904468-07-1	*How Good is your Pot-Limit Omaha?*	Stewart Reuben
1-904468-20-9	*Poker on the Internet (2nd edition)*	Andrew Kinsman
1-904468-15-2	*How Good is your Limit Hold'em?*	Byron Jacobs/Jim Brier

D & B Bridge

1-904468-09-8	*Defensive Plays*	Sally Brock
1-904468-00-4	*No Trump Contracts*	David Bird
1-904468-01-2	*Suit Contracts*	Brian Senior
1-904468-14-4	*Concise Bridge*	Sally Brock

D & B Puzzles

1-904468-03-9	*200 Word Puzzles*	Carter and Russell
1-904468-02-0	*400 IQ Puzzles*	Carter and Russell
1-904468-10-1	*How to Solve IQ Puzzles*	Carter and Russell
1-904468-11-X	*How to Solve Word Puzzles*	Carter and Russell
1-904468-05-5	*The Times Two Brains*	Keene and Jacobs

Other D & B Books

1-904468-13-6	*Gambling Online*	Angus Dunnington
1-904468-18-7	*Boost Your Interview Test Performance*	Philip Carter

D & B Publishing, PO Box 18, Hassocks, West Sussex BN6 9WR, UK
Tel: 01273 834680, Fax: 01273 831629,
E-mail: info@dandbpublishing.com, Website: www.dandbpublishing.com

The function between brain cells where communication crosses is called the synapse. In the synapse, an electrical impulse shunts chemical messengers between two brain cells, transmitting thought. No one knows how this is done.

Your body provides your brain with information through a network of 500,000 touch detectors; and four million pair sensitive structures.

The number of neurons or nerve cells in your brain is approximately 12 trillion (more than two and a half thousand times the number of people currently living on the planet)

The brain is about the size of two clenched fists and, on average, weighs an incredibly light 3lb (1.4kg).

Through your olfactory system (your nose!) your brain is able to detect one molecule of 'smell' in one part per trillion of air.

The brain consumes 20 per cent of the body's oxygen system.

Within your brain there is enough atomic energy to build any of the world's cities many times.

Your brain is the only living part of the body that cannot feel pain.

Your brain listens with your ears. These both contain 24,000 fibres that are able to detect enormous ranges and subtle distinctions in the air's molecular

The left brain, the centre of logical thought, controls the right hand and vice versa. Since the right brain is stronger in visual skills, it is perhaps hardly surprising that left-handedness is roughly twice as common among artists.

Your brain cells contain 1,000 trillion trillion protein molecules. Each brain cell has the physical possibility of connecting with 100,000 adjoining brain cells.

Every day your brain makes more connections than the world's telephone system.

First published in 2005 by D & B Publishing,
PO Box 18, Hassocks, West Sussex BN6 9WR

British Library Cataloguing-in-Publication Data
A catalogue record for this book is available from the British Library.

ISBN 1-904468-15-2

All sales enquiries should be directed to:
D & B Publishing, PO Box 18, Hassocks, West Sussex BN6 9WR, UK
Tel: +44 (0)1273 834680; Fax: +44 (0)1273 831629
e-mail: info@dandbpublishing.com,
Website: www.dandbpublishing.com

*This book is dedicated to Dr. Mahathir Mohamad, former Prime Minister of Malaysia
and sponsor of the World Memory Championships in Kuala Lumpur 2003.*

The term and concept Mind Map™ as referred to in this book is
a registered trademark.

Cover design by Horacio Monteverde
Production by Navigator Guides
Printed and bound in the UK by Biddles Ltd.

CONTENTS

INTERNATIONAL PANEL
OF EXPERTS

The authors would like to thank the following who comprise the International Panel of Experts who made valuable contributions to this book:

Blackstock, Les – Former European Shogi Champion
Bond, Philip – World Record holder matrix memorisation of Pi
Brock, Sally – International Bridge player, bridge author and journalist
Chambers, Philip – World Memory Council
Day, Chris – World Memory Council
Divinsky, Professor Nathan– Professor in the Statistics Department of the University of British Columbia in Vancouver
Docherty, Ian – Memory expert
Fairbairn, John – Shogi author and expert
Fortman, Richard – Draughts Grandmaster
Graham, John – former Bridge correspondent of *The Times*
Money, Paul – International Backgammon player and author
O'Brien, Dominic – Multiple winner World Memory Championship
Pask, Richard – Draughts Grandmaster
Pridmore, Ben – World Memory Champion 2004-2005
Pritchard, David – author of *Encyclopaedia of Chess Variants*
Schaeffer, Jonathan – chief programmer Chinook draughts program
Simpole, Julian – Vice President of the Commonwealth Chess Association and former editor of *Synapsia Magazine*
Timmins, Brian – English Go Association
Wade, Bob OBE – Chess Master and chief national chess coach
Wedd, Nick – Go expert
Wilshire, Kenneth – Bronze Medallist, 1st World Memory Championship
Woo, David – Chinese Chess Institute, San Francisco

Acknowledgements

The authors would also like to thank Robert Parsons of the Royal College of Heralds, Hardinge Simpole Publishing, *Synapsia Magazine* and the cartoonist Pécub.

FOREWORD

Citius, Altius, Fortius

Faster, higher, stronger – the Olympic motto. But there are limitations to what the physical can achieve before the body cracks up. For those of you who have enjoyed the thrill of being terrified by science fiction or fantasy monsters such as the 60 foot spider, take heart from the fact that this is an anatomical impossibility. Come a certain size and the body of a super-arachnid would simply implode. Then again, the four-minute mile created a furore when this important barrier was first broken. Since those heady days, however, progress in speed running over middle distances has become tectonic. With the human body designed as it now is, a one-minute mile is patently not possible. Of course, over the future aeons of Darwinian evolution, the human body may develop wheels, thus solving the *citius* problem at a stroke, but we are certainly very distant from such fantasmagorical speculations.

No Limits

However, in the realm of the mental, the topic of this book, there are, believe it or not, virtually no limits. Try imagining, for example, a very large amount of money which you would like to be yours. It does not take long to multiply this sum by ten, or a hundred or a million – the human brain is the most complicated entity known to humankind, far outstripping distant galaxies in the complexity of its organisation. Hence, where the body, seen from the perspective of its physical limits, may be restricted, the mind is free to soar to infinity.

Vital Statistics

Dominic O'Brien has been known to memorise a random set of numbers perfectly – the numbers are read out and after a pause Dominic recalls them with no errors. And how many numbers does he juggle and order in his mind in such sequences? Try it for yourself: is it a few familiar telephone numbers' worth strung together?; is it in the tens or twenties? No! Dominic, many times World Memory Champion can access hundreds of spoken numbers with perfect recall – a mind blowing feat, to put it mildly.

Or take chess – a miniature game of chess lasts 25 moves (on each side) before a result is achieved. Grandmaster games often last for 40 moves or more. Let us say that we wish to write down and record for posterity all miniature games of chess, and store them in books and print equal to the London telephone directory or the Parisian annuaire. A question we love posing to the uninitiated is – how much space do you have to reserve to store the books?

The most popular answer is 'the Albert Hall'. Sorry, way off! The correct response, confirmed by Professor Nathan Divinsky of the Maths and Statistics Department of the University of British Columbia, is staggering: first fill all available space between earth and the furthest known galaxy, building outwards as a giant ball in space, not once but ten to the power of twenty times – and that is just the short games. Yet grandmasters can regularly play 100 games or more at the same time, hold their own with computers which can calculate billions of positions per second or even take on multiple opponents without sight of the pieces and boards.

Instant Access

Chess grandmasters can also glance at a position from a game and reconstruct almost perfectly a board crowded with pieces after a mere microseconds observation. This applies essentially to positions from games with an internal logic and structure of their own – fling the pieces at random on the board and the task immediately becomes more difficult – but not impossible.

In 1991, at the time of the first World Memory Championship, a shuffled pack of cards could be memorised and recalled accurately after around five minutes cogitation. Experts promptly pronounced this to be near the limit of human capacity. A decade and a half later the recall of a complete shuffled pack is down to around 30 seconds. However, is it possible that memorisers might be able – like chess grandmasters – to remember an entire shuffled pack simply by looking at them for a second, spread out on a table, rather then picking through the pack card by card? It would have to start with the order and logic of a bridge hand, perhaps, but who knows where it could lead from that point of embarkation?

The Mental Giants

So, this is the world which we now invite you to enter – the world of colossal mental feats, performed by such giants as Dr. Marion Tinsley who dominated international draughts for decades and whose losses could be numbered on the fingers of two hands; of Garry Kasparov, a man able to defeat national squads of opposing chess grandmasters simultaneously under pressure from the constantly ticking clock; or Dominic O'Brien, whose exploits confounded the conventional psychological wisdom of the 20th century. Yet none of these were freaks or prodigies of nature, born with two heads or an extra brain hidden beneath the gluteus maximus – all were or are – talented intellectuals who formed a dream and pursued it with unquenchable determination. doubtless they would have succeeded in whatever field to which their ambition led them – as can you.

Serious Money

One mind sport which has witnessed an explosion of interest in recent years is Poker. This has been fuelled by the arrival of online cardrooms on the internet and there are now thousands of cash games and tournaments available 24 hours a day at hundreds of different sites. The incredible interest that these generate can be seen from the valuation of nearly $5 billion which was attached to the leading online site, PartyPoker.com, when it floated in 2005.

The 'World Championship' of the poker world is the World Series, which is held every summer in Las Vegas. In this event, players 'buy-in' with $10,000 and the accumulation of these entry fees makes up the prize pool. When a player loses their chips they are eliminated and play continues until one player has all the money. Prizes are typically paid out to the top 10% on a sliding scale with the winner receiving the lion's share.

In 2001, this event had 613 entries and the eventual winner, Juan Carlos Mortensen of Madrid, took home $1.5 million. The runner-up won just over $1 million. This was fairly typical of this tournament at the time. However, with the advent of on-line play it is now possible to enter qualifiers and, by winning such an event, a player gets a prize of a 'free' buy-in to the World Series. These events have proved to be enormously popular and, in consequence, entries for the World Series have increased dramatically.

In 2003, there were 839 entries and the eventual winner was the wonderfully-named Chris Moneymaker of the US, who took home $2.5 million. The remarkable feature of his achievement was that this was the very first 'live' tournament he had played and that he obtained his seat by winning a $40 qualifier on the internet!

By 2004 things had really taken off and at the start of play there were an astonishing 2,576 competitors – three times the number from the previous year. The winner was Greg Raymer of the US, who scooped $5 million for his victory. He was also an internet qualifier. Even the player finishing in fifth place took home over $1 million.

This year (2005) saw 5,661 entrants for the World Series with total prize money at nearly $53 million. This is, by far, the biggest ever prize fund for a sporting event. The winner, Joseph Hachem, walked away with $7.5 million, with the runner-up, Steve Dannenmann netting $4.5 million. Everyone who made it through to the last day's play and final table (9 players) pocketed a minimum of $1 million. Presumably it will not be long before the total prize money tops $100 million.

INTRODUCTION

THE INEVITABLE GROWTH OF MIND SPORTS

The Birth of Mind Sports

Since the dawn of civilisation, some ten thousand years ago, history has recorded that men and women have been games players. The earliest writings of ancient civilisations regularly make reference to games similar in concept to tic-tac-toe (noughts and crosses). Something like Draughts was played in Ancient Egypt and Go was referred to in Chinese texts of about 1000BC as a game that any reader would know.

Chess is said to have originated in India around AD 600 under the name *chaturanga*, a word describing the four traditional army units of Indian military forces: foot soldiers (pawns), cavalry (knights), chariots (rooks) and elephants (today's bishops). Since 1970s, however, more and more weight has been given to the idea that China already had a version of Chess before India. There were mentions of Xiang Qi (Chinese Chess) in documents during the Warring States period (403-221BC).

Confucius is said to have known Go. To Plato, games were a vital part of a leader's training. Board games have been portrayed by artists through the centuries, from Ancient Greece and Rome to the illuminated manuscripts of medieval monks and the modern art of Ernst and Duchamp. To all of them, the games had a mystical significance.

These ancient games now take their part in Olympiads alongside modern inventions ranging from Abalone to Zatre. Old and new, however, they share one element: the power to hone the mind.

The First Great Mind Sportsman: As-Suli (AD 854-946)

Mind sports play a vital part in the lives of many geniuses and, of the various occidental mind sports, chess is the king. It is the one practised most widely and has the most well-documented and carefully written theory to back it up. A number of the geniuses have rated chess highly.

Goethe called the game 'the touchstone of the intellect'. Haroun Al-Raschid, the Abbasyd Caliph of Islam (AD 786-809), the man idealized in the Arabian Nights, was the first of his dynasty to play chess. The 11th-century Byzantine Emperor, Alexius Comnenus, was allegedly playing chess when surprised by a murderous conspiracy, which being a good chess player he managed to escape!

The Aladdin of the fairy tale was, in real life, a chess player, a lawyer from Samarkand in the court of Tamburlaine. Tamburlaine himself loved to play chess and named his son Shah Rukh, since Tamburlaine was moving a Rook at the time the birth was announced. Another genius, Benjamin Franklin, was an enthusiastic chess player – indeed the first chess publication in America was Franklin's *Morals of Chess* which appeared in 1786. Chess was mentioned by Shakespeare, Goethe, Leibniz and Einstein. Ivan the Terrible, Queen Elizabeth I, Catherine the Great and Napoleon all played chess.

A Cradle For Genius

However, the first Chess Grandmaster, the first mental sportsman, the first genius of mind sports, was the Baghdad chess player As-Suli. It is diffiicult for Western audiences to grasp that Baghdad, As-Suli's home city, was once the world capital of chess; indeed it was the capital of the world for some time from the 9th century onwards. Baghdad was founded in AD 762 by the Caliph Al-Mansour, who employed 100,000 men to build it. This circular city, with a diameter of 8655 ft (2638 m) and surrounded by a rampart of no fewer than 360 towers, almost immediately proved to be too small for the burgeoning population. By the time of the Caliph Haroun Al-Raschid, Baghdad had expanded, taking in quarters for commerce and artisans, and by AD 814 it was the world's largest city. The stupendous growth of Baghdad was a most astonishing global phenomenon. By 814 it covered an area approximately 40 square miles (100 square kilometres) – the equivalent of modern day Paris within the outer boulevards. Baghdad was the dominant city of the world and As-Suli was the multi-talented mind sportsman, poet, politician, and Chess Grandmaster who exemplified the pre-eminent culture of Baghdad at that time. Baghdad dwarfed all other world cities, and in terms of culture, art, scientific investigation and chess, it was the most convincing and powerful testament to the astonishing force of Islam.

Theory And Analysis

In the 9th and 10th centuries chess was known in the Arabic tongue as *Shatranj*, and Baghdad was to Shatranj what Moscow became to the modern game – the world capital of chess. Baghdad was a cultured flourishing centre packed with chess grandmasters and chess theoreticians, who wrote volume after volume about critical positions and chess opening theory. The main differences between Shatranj and chess as we now know it, which was developed during the Renaissance in the 15th century, was that in the old game of Shatranj, a win could be achieved by taking all of your opponent's pieces, apart from his king. You did not need to force checkmate. The queen, known as the Visier, was a comparatively helpless piece, only able to move one square diagonally in each direction, whereas today it is the most powerful piece on the chess board.

The First Mind Sportsman

Like the reigning modern World number one, Garry Kasparov, As-Suli came from an area bordering the Caspian Sea and, as a young man, he travelled to the capital to become the chess favourite of the political leader of his day, the Caliph Al-Muktafi. But in AD 940 As-Suli uttered an indiscreet political comment, and had to flee from Baghdad. He died soon afterwards in Basra at the grand old age of 92.

The Chess Puzzle Which Defied Solution For 1000 Years

A chess genius lives on in his published studies and puzzles. As-Suli set one puzzle which he described as: 'Old, very old and extremely difficult to solve. Nobody could solve it or say whether it was a draw or win. In fact there is no man on earth who can solve it if I, As-Suli, have not shown him the solution'. This was his proud boast and it held good until only very recently, when modern Grandmasters armed with computers finally cracked the puzzle.

Versatility

As-Suli was the strongest player of his time, a composer of chess puzzles, and the author of the first book describing a systematic way of playing Shatranj. For more than 600 years after his death, the highest praise an Arab could bestow on a chess player was to say that he played like As-Suli – he won every chess match that he has known to have contested. As-Suli was a resident at the court of the Caliph where his reputation was that of an excellent conversationalist with immense encyclopedic knowledge. He owned an enormous library, and wrote many history books as well as his two text books on chess. He was also a great teacher of the game – the next great Arabic player of Shatranj, Al-Lajlaj, was one of his pupils.

Symbol of Intelligence

As-Suli can be seen as a symbol of the great Islamic culture that flourished in Baghdad, possessing great qualities of mind, thought and intellect at a time when Europe itself was plunged in the Dark Ages and much of the world was in chaos. His was a pinnacle of sophistication and culture not to be attained by others for many centuries.

The Development of Mind Sports

The trend of the growth of games over the centuries has been a fascinating one. Interestingly, all major games have followed an identical growth pattern:

Stage 1: A single originator or small group of originators come up with a new creative idea for a game testing mental skills.

Stage 2: The new game is introduced to a wider range of players, and a small band of cognoscenti forms a loosely knit group of players.

Stage 3: The loosely knit group becomes an informal 'club'.

Stage 4: The club becomes more formalised, and multiplies, giving birth to other clubs similar in form to the original.

Stage 5: Players emerge who become the recognised leaders, experts and theorists of the game.

Stage 6: Formal competitions are organised, and local champions appear.

Stage 7: Literature is produced on the background and theory of the game, and formalised rules become established game-law.

Stage 8: National and international competitions arise, and a World Champion is crowned. Concurrent with this stage is the proliferation of articles, magazines and books on the subject, and the evolution of different 'schools' of thought on the game.

A natural limitation to the growth of games in the past has been the fact that in most instances the number of players is two, occasionally three or four, and rarely more. Unlike a physical sporting event the diminutive size of the board usually limits spectatorship to a handful.

Contrast this with the number of spectators in the Roman Colosseum or the modern sports stadium, and we can readily see one of the reasons for the historical dominance of physical sports over mental games as spectator events.

Despite these limiting barriers to the growth of Mind Sports as spectator events, the expansion in recent years has been staggering. The game of Chess, once perceived as a contest for old men with grey beards, first hit the front page headlines in 1972 when the mercurial American genius Bobby Fischer wrested the World Championship crown from Russia's Boris Spassky in Reykjavik. Since then, Chess and its most prominent personalities have increasingly become media stars.

A measure of the growth of interest in Mind Sports is reflected in the increased prize fund for major contests. In 1969 the World Chess Championship match was worth around 3,000 roubles (less than $3,000) to the winner. In 1993 Kasparov and Short contested a purse of £1.7 million, considerably in excess of the top two prizes at Wimbledon or any golf tournament. The Fischer-Spassky match of 1992 attracted an even larger prize fund, namely $5 million.

Concurrent with the explosion of interest in Mind Sports, is a similar explosion of interest in measuring mental skills, competing in them, and forming organisations based on them. Witness the dramatic growth of Mensa, the high IQ society, whose membership in England alone increases by over 2,000 per year, that membership having as one of its major hobbies the playing of thinking games and the solving of thinking puzzles.

This newly accelerating growth of interest in the mental arena has reached an explosion point. Local, national and international competitions proliferate; virtually all important newspapers and magazines carry articles, columns and feature sections on Chess, Bridge, crosswords and brain-twisters. Other popular columns include Scrabble, Backgammon and Poker.

This increase has been fuelled by the internet and it is now possible to play almost any game against opponents from all over the world at any time. However, not all the competition is virtual. Hundreds, in some cases a thousand or more competitors descend on towns and cities for Scrabble, Monopoly, Go, Chess, Bridge and other championships, and the demand for literature, clubs, playing venues and competitions increases steadily.

What Makes a Mind Sports Champion?

The qualities that make a mind sports champion are virtually identical to those that make a are found in anybody who excels in any field. Ten main attributes stand out from a number of others, and we will concentrate on these here. The reader is encouraged to compare these qualities with those of the great champions in chess, the great champions in other fields, and perhaps even the readers' own 'Olympian' qualities!

The major traits that identify the personality of a champion are:

1 Vision

The degree to which the goal of becoming champion is absolute, imaginatively seen, precisely formulated, clearly stated, and comprehensively understood. 'it is the 'guiding light' of the individual (or team).

One of the 'greatest of all time' in this department was he who is famous for that very quote – Muhammad Ali. His visions of victory were so complete that he would describe in detail, the round by round progress of many of his fights, culminating in the round and type of victory, four months before the fight. Not only were his predictions eerily accurate, they were so strong and so perfectly described that his opponents shared his vision for the fight!

2 Commitment

This combines the desire to win, and the faith in the self that the goal of becoming champion can be attained. Interestingly, most world champions usually stated their commitment publicly, wrote it down as a personal incentive, or did both. Bobby Fischer is often cited as the most committed to becoming World Champion the world has ever known. From a country with only a very few top-rated players at the time, Bobby single-handedly took on the combined might of the Soviet chess machine, having to play against not only the nine other strongest players in the world, but also their combined team tactics against him in tournaments.

One of the most insightful quotes on commitment comes from the world record holder in Used Human Vocabulary, Goethe (50,000 words; 210 IQ), who said:

'Whatever you can do or dream you can, begin it. Boldness has genius, power and magic in it. Begin it now.'

3 Persistence

Most of the all-time great champions were capable of continuing the pursuit of their goals both in the face of adversity and when others had given up. Tremendous persistence was also demonstrated by the great American Draughts/Checkers World Champion (a fifty-year reign), Dr Marion Tinsley. He played for eight hours a day, five days a week, for two weeks, against the implacable Chinook computer (the world's official number two player, capable of calculating three million moves a second, and with a database of 27 billion positions) and crushed it in the final game, leaping from his chair and proclaiming 'A victory for human beings!' And gymnast Peter Vidmar, the Olympic Gold Medallist and Olympic Gold Medal team captain, ascribed his Gold Medals to the ability to practice that one minute more, try just that little bit harder, continue just that little bit longer than anyone else'.

4 Learning from Mistakes and Overcoming Fear

The lesser competitor will become dispirited by mistakes, losses and failure. The great champions study the reasons why and come back improved. Witness for example Greg Norman's performance in the final round of the 1993 British Open, described as one of the greatest final rounds in history. The Sunday Times reported: 'Norman, however, turned every negative into a positive, as though crushing defeats were essential pieces in the jigsaw of great golf. 'The whole crux is that you believe in yourself. I can bounce back from whatever they throw at me,' said Norman. 'The appropriate attitude to the enormous danger of fear, and the overcoming of it, was succinctly expressed and summarised in the 'obliteration of obliteration' mantra by the psychologist and author Frank Herbert in his famous novel *Dune*:

'Fear is the little-death that brings total obliteration. I will face my fear. I will permit it to pass over me and through me. And when it has gone past I will turn the inner eye to see its path.

Where the fear has gone there will be nothing.

Only I will remain.'

5 Knowledge

An intimate, detailed and comprehensive subject knowledge is a pre-requisite for a World Champion. Michael Schumacher is renowned for knowing more about Formula One cars than most team engineers; and Lennox Lewis (also a keen chessplayer) has an encyclopaedic knowledge of boxing history.

6 Mental Literacy

This refers to general and particular knowledge and application of information about the brain's skills and how to use and get the most from them. These include imagination, logic, rhythm, analysis, spatial awareness, number, associative power, memory, intuition and creativity. Contrary to popular beliefs, chess champions (as will be shown) and physical champions share these same attributes. Dominic O'Brien, the former World Memory Champion, practices mental and physical skills for a minimum of four hours per day, taking himself for walks and runs in the morning on which he applies every facet of his mind to the perception imaging and remembering of multiple loci, pathways and maps in his mind.

The reader is invited to search for a physical sport in which the application of a majority of these Mental Literacy attributes would not be advantageous.

7 Positive Attitude

The mental attitude of the champion tends to be realistically positive, enthusiastic, optimistic, up-beat and open to every opportunity for getting the best out of any situation. Examples abound, including Muhammad Ali (Boxing), Chionofuji (Sumo Wrestling), Daley Thompson (Decathlon), Steven Hendry (Snooker), Steve Ovett and Sally Gunnell (Athletics), Mark Spitz (Swimming) and Joe Montana (American Football).

It is interesting to note here that Nigel Short, not often thought of as either athletic or interested in sport, has as one of his major role-models the greatest Sumo wrestler of all time, Chionofuji who himself broke all the traditions of the sport by becoming the smallest Grand Champion and by transforming Sumo from a sport dominated by weight and strength to one dominated by an insatiable desire to win, a new and creative approach, and speed of both body and mind.

8 The Master Mind Group

The psychology of the champion is reflected in the degree of excellence in the quality of the individuals who make up the immediate personal and professional 'circle of advisors' -those individuals who actively assist in achieving the champion's visions and goals. This is one area where even great champions can reveal their Achilles Heel witness again Mike Tyson.

9 Love of the Game

In the champions this is expressed as an all consuming passion and enthusiasm for not only the particular task/game/competition at hand, but also the wider implications and applications of the field. Great champions and leaders often go on to become great teachers and promoters of their sport.

Both Billie-Jean King and Martina Navratilova, the longest reigning and most titled players in women's tennis history, when asked how they were able to maintain their standards for so long, both answered with the question 'why should it be so difficult to continue playing for so long, when we love the game so much?'

10 Energy

Without exception, 'The Greats' were and are known to exude energy; physical, sensual and sexual (the recently 'exposed' peccadilloes of Einstein may perhaps be seen in a different light!). The current number one Kasparov's energy and persistence are extraordinary.

CHAPTER ONE

MENTAL WORLD RECORDS:
THE STORY BEGINS...

In this chapter we give the history of some mental world records, as well as introducing early attempts to enter the record books by some of the growing brigade of international brain stars.

Memorising Pi

Pi is one of those rare numbers whose digits follow no known pattern of duplication. With its length apparently infinite, the possibilities it offers have caused it to become such a popular target for memory record breakers that it has become a field of its own.

Ben Pridmore is the current World Memory Champion. Here is his own personal account of the battles memorisers have had with this number.

Irrational

π, or pi, is the 16th letter of the Greek alphabet. It's also the symbol used to represent the number that you get when you divide the length of the circumference (the line around the outside) of a circle by the diameter (a straight line across the middle).

Pi is what mathematicians call an 'irrational' number. This means that it can't be expressed as the result of one whole number divided by another. In other words, it goes on and on forever, an endless string of random numbers after the decimal point. A computer in Japan is currently dedicated to calculating pi to more and more decimal places – it is currently up to around one and a half trillion.

Pi has also for some reason always been regarded as the ultimate test of memory, perhaps because it's so random and arbitrary that it sets a test that nobody could argue is unfair. In the olden days, it used to be cool if you could recite a mere couple of hundred digits. In 1973, the world record was 930. Then in the mid 70s, the whole idea really took off, and a series of people took it into the thousands and then the ten-thousands. Hideaki Tomoyori of Japan recited 20,000 digits in 1979, and Creighton Carvello did 20,013 the following year, which took a while to beat. Since then the records have been:

No. of digits	Memoriser (country)	Year
31,811	Rajan Mahadevan (India)	1985
40,000	Hideaki Tomoyori (Japan)	1987
42,195	Hiroyuki Goto (Japan)	1995
83,431	Akira Haraguchi (Japan)	2005

There are other records involving pi, which I think were dreamed up mainly to circumvent the sheer length of time it takes to recite so many numbers. There's the 'pi matrix' record, in which the digits of pi are arranged in numbered lines of 50, and the memoriser has to recall all the digits of any given line. Or there's the test involving breaking pi into five-digit strings, telling the memorizer one of these and asking them to name the two strings on either side. But the real Everest is to memorise a huge number of digits and recite them out loud, without mistakes, all at once.

I decided to try to beat the record mainly as a compromise. After winning the World Memory Championship in 2004, I had a lot of trouble motivating myself to keep practicing. Having spent four years working towards winning it, I just wasn't all that excited by the idea of trying to win it again. So, rather than give up memory altogether, I decided to try a different challenge, one that would keep my mental muscles in shape for when I was more in the mood for the WMC and give me a chance to try something new.

Long-term memorising of a huge number of digits of pi is a different kind of task entirely from the short-term memorising of a mere couple of thousand for immediate recall. If I'd sat down and thought about it a bit more before I started, I would have done things a bit differently, but the way I went about it was essentially the same way I approach the hour numbers event at the WMC.

Mental Journeys

I dreamed up 50 mental journeys of 111 points each, converted each group of three digits to an image of an object or person and placed three of these images at each point on the route. The first single digit of each thousand I memorised in a separate string, so that I could find a starting point more easily if someone asked me what the 37,459th digit was.

What I should have done is create an image for each four-digit number. The only reason I don't use that system for the World Championships is because there isn't enough recall time to go over a list of 10,000 images, but that isn't a problem with long-term, unlimited-time memory like this. That would have reduced the amount of mental information I needed to process, avoided repetition of images (each of the 1,000 images I used occurs between six and thirty-one times in the 50,000 digits) and made the whole thing a bit easier. Ah well, maybe I'll do that next time I try something like this.

I don't think there's really any limit to the number of digits of pi a human being can memorise, given the time to do it. I firmly believe that the brain has a nearly infinite capacity for memory, more than we can ever use up in a lifetime anyway, and it's just a matter of learning how to use it properly. The only problem comes with whether anyone can be bothered to spend all that time reciting it. Saying 50,000 digits is going to take me at least six hours, and I talk quite quickly. There's really no way to break the record without it going on all day. But I'm confident that the record will continue to be broken. I'm expecting to see someone do 100,000 digits in my lifetime.

Pi Trivia

In the entirely arbitrary way I divided pi into three-digit numbers, the combination 550 occurs the least frequently. And on three of those six occurrences it's immediately preceded by 458.

The 50,001st digit is 3. But I'm not going to recite that; I'll stop at a round number.

Of the first 50,000 digits after the decimal point, there are 5055 1s, 5052 5's, 5033 0's, 5030 8's, 5018 6's, 5011 4's, 5010 9's, 4977 7's, 4947 3's and only 4867 2's.

There's only one string of six consecutive identical digits in the first 50,000, and it happens only 726 places in, with six nines in a row.

The first 0 in the expansion doesn't occur until the 32nd digit after the decimal point.

If you had a circle whose diameter was the length of the entire universe, and you wanted to know the circumference exact to within one angstrom (the smallest unit of measurement there is), 35 decimal places of pi would suffice. Measuring distances more accurate than that would be pointless, because there aren't any perfect circles once you get down to the atoms – they're lumpy and irregular.

Chess

Chessplayers are ranked according to gradings devised by the World Chess Federation (FIDE). A moderate club player would have a ranking of between 1000 to 1200; a class 'A' player a ranking of 1800+; an expert a ranking of 2200+; an International Master a ranking of 2400+; and a top ranking International Grandmaster a ranking of over 2700.

The current World Champion, and indeed the chessplayer with the all-time highest ranking, is Garry Kasparov with a ranking of 2815. Kasparov is a particularly good example of a well rounded and integrated, holanthropic human being. His friends describe him as a cultivated and curious man who closely follows literature, film and politics. To keep his brain in shape he keeps his body in shape. He runs, swims, cycles and plays soccer as part of his training programme for World Championship matches. Kasparov makes full use of the range of his mental skills while playing. He is described as the artist of the chessboard, taking bold chances, making breathtaking sacrifices and hunting for the opponent's king with passion. 'From the very beginning of a game, I strive to make it as sharp as possible and to take it outside the familiar patterns,' he once said.

Speed Reading

Speed reading tests are primarily based on the reading of novels. The reader has to read an entire novel as fast as possible, subsequently giving a presentation to people who have already read the novel in depth. This presentation has to include knowledgeable comments about and integration of the following main areas: characters, setting, plot, philosophy, symbolism, language level, literary style, metaphor, themes and historical context.

The world's fastest reader on record to date is Sean Adam with a reading speed of 3,850 words per minute. In a subsequent questioning session, Sean Adam was able to answer every question that was asked of him by others who had read the book. The top ten world rankings for speed reading are as follows:

	Speed Reader (country)	Words Per Minute
1	Sean Adam (USA)	3,850
2	Kjetill Gunnarson (Norway)	3,050
3	Vanda North (England)	3,000
4	Anne Jones (England)	2,246
5	Mithymna Corke (Netherlands)	2,100
6	Mithymna Corke (Netherlands)	2,100
7	Luc van Hof (Netherlands)	1,906
8	Michael Gelb (USA)	1,805
9	Cinnamon Adam (USA)	1,782
10	James Longworth (England)	1,750

Creativity

Creativity is defined by Torrance, the doyen of creativity testing, as follows: 'Creativity is a process of becoming sensitive to problems, deficiencies, gaps in knowledge, missing elements, disharmonies and so on; identifying the difficulty; searching for solutions; making guesses or formulating hypotheses about the deficiencies; testing and re-testing these hypotheses and possibly modifying and re-testing them; and finally communicating the results.'

Torrance Tests of creative thinking were developed to assess the process and especially the ability of the subject to think divergently and originally. Such tests also challenge the test-taker not only to find a solution, but actually to invent the problem to which he or she will provide a solution. The success of the test-taker will express itself through the divergent thinking factors of fluency; flexibility; originality and elaboration. It is argued that every creative production is at the same time the result and manifestation of these four factors of divergent thinking.

Fluency reflects the test-taker's ability to produce large numbers of ideas with words (verbal fluency) or with pictures (figural fluency). Quantity or ease with which associations flow is the main characteristic.

Flexibility represents the test-taker's ability to produce different kinds of ideas; the ability to shift from one approach to another raising a rich variety of strategies.

Originality represents the ability to produce ideas that are unusual, unique, and far removed from what is normal or commonplace. A person scoring high in originality may be perceived as non-conforming, but this does not mean that such a person is either erratic or impulsive. On the contrary, originality is the result of considerable 'controlled' intellectual energy, and generally a capacity for high levels of concentration.

According to Torrance, high scores on *elaboration* indicate that the subject is able to develop, embroider, embellish, carry out or otherwise elaborate ideas. Such persons are likely to demonstrate keenness or sensitivity in observation.

Normal scores in the verbal scale are:

Fluency	77
Flexibility	27
Originality	37

The highest registered scores in the world to date were achieved by co-author Tony Buzan: Fluency 249, Flexibility 94 and Originality 368. Throughout the test Tony also achieved an originality score on the figural scale of 100%.

Creativity, like any other mental skill, can be taught and learned. In preparation for his Torrance test, Tony Buzan, like Kasparov, trained himself physically, and honed his Mind Mapping and memory skills before breaking the world record.

Mind Mapping as an Aid to Memory, Creativity and IQ

Mind Mapping is a simple, practical tool that can help you:

- Think faster and more creatively
- Get more work done in less time
- Improve your memory
- Plan projects, prepare presentations, run meetings and solve problems with ease

A Mind Map is a simple, easy way to represent your thoughts using key words, colours and imagery. Its non-linear format encourages you to begin generating ideas immediately and allows you to put a tremendous amount of significant information on one piece of paper. Mapping integrates your logical and imaginative thinking to increase your productivity.

Mind Mapping was developed in the early 1970's by co-author and brain researcher Tony Buzan as a whole-brain alternative to outlining. It makes it easier to access the tremendous creative potential of your brain.

Uses of Mind Maps

Mind Mapping is a powerful tool for improving your effectiveness in planning, remembering and communicating. Mind Mapping improves:

Planning

Meetings

Conferences

Presentations

Budgets

Strategic vision

Projects

Brainstorming sessions

Performance appraisals

World Mind Mapping Championship Rankings

Position	Name	Medals
1	Elaine Colliar (Scotland)	5 golds
2	Phil Chambers (England)	2 golds, 1 silver, 1 bronze
3	Kevin Dalley (England)	2 silvers

Art

Fastest Artist in the World

Ripley's Believe It Or Not Museum Display contains 'fast' paintings, and videos showing how they were created as recognisable landscapes. The world record holder is Conni Gordon of Miami Beach, Florida, who completed such a painting in less than one minute.

Most People taught Art in the World

This record is held by the person who has been proved to have taught more people to create art (paintings) than anyone else in the world. The world record holder is, once again Conni Gordon – over sixteen million people taught in 40 years.

Intelligence Quotient (IQ)

IQ is a concept that is often mistakenly assumed to have begun with a desire to limit peoples' freedom by classifying their intellectual capacity. Nothing could be further from the truth. In the early part the last century, a Frenchman, Stanford Binet, observed that virtually all students attending universities were from the upper classes. Feeling this to be intrinsically unfair, he attempted to devise tests that would be 'class free', and that would enable any child to advance through the academic system on intellectual merit alone. In a work of deep social conscience and considerable intellectual rigour, he selected basic abilities such as vocabulary knowledge, ability to manipulate numbers and short-term memory, testing massive sections of the population in each of these skills. Those who scored averagely for any age group were given a score of 100, those scoring below or above being given scores below or above 100 depending on how far they were from average. Thus a score of 70 was particularly low, a score of 130 especially high (in the 'genius' range).

Only in the last few decades has the IQ test begun to form, against the obvious wishes of its originator, its own class system. For a number of years it has been assumed that intelligence quotients are a reflection of an innate ability and are unchanging. Work by many researchers has shown that the IQ score can be seen much like a high-jump bar. Whatever score you achieve may be considered the 'height you can jump at the moment'. With appropriate training your score can go, should you wish, either down or up!

The current world record holder in the two very important IQ categories of vocabulary and recognition and manipulation of similarities, is Brain Club member Sean Adam with Weschler scores of 152, translated into Catell scores of 180. These scores are the maximum available for the test.

Who were the Greatest Historical IQ's?

The most in-depth work on this topic appears so far to have been done by C.M.Cox, who wrote in *Genetic Studies of Genius* (1923) about historical figures and their probable IQ's. Cox had five different psychometricians estimate the IQ of the historical great brains on the basis of biographical data between their ages of 17 and 26. Cox then averaged the scores of the five psychometricians, and using his own psychometric and historical knowledge, presented an estimate of their most probable IQ's.

Top IQ's of the Great Brains (according to C.M.Cox)

Ran	Name	IQ		Rank	Name	IQ
1	Goethe	210		15-17	Coleridge	175
2	Leibnitz	205		15-17	J.Q.Adams	175
3-4	Newton	190		15-17	Kant	175
3-4	Pitt (younger)	190		18-21	Tennyson	170
5	Galileo	185		18-21	Faraday	170
6-14	da Vinci	180		18-21	Handel	170
6-14	J.S.Mill	180		18-21	Raphael	170
6-14	Hume	180		22-27	Wordsworth	165
6-14	Erasmus	180		22-27	Sam.Johnson	165
6-14	Descartes	180		22-27	J.S.Bach	165
6-14	Bacon	180		22-27	Disraeli	165
6-14	Dickens	180		22-27	Mozart	165
6-14	Milton	180		22-27	D.Webster	165
6-14	Michelangelo	180		28	Rembrandt	155

The scale by which Cox measured these IQ's would have the top 2% threshold (eligibility for entering Mensa) as an IQ score of 138.

In order to judge how frequently the all-time top scores would occur in the human population, the following table is provided:

IQ	Ratio in Population
150	1 out of 300
160	1 out of 3,000
170	1 out of 30,000
180	1 out of 100,000
190	1 out of 1,000,000
200	1 out of 10,000,000

Our own conclusions on the record historical IQ's are as follows:

Top IQ's of the Great Brains

(according to Tony Buzan and Raymond Keene in *Buzan's Book of Genius*)

Rank	Name	IQ		Rank	Name	IQ
1	da Vinci	220		8	Archimedes	190
2	Goethe	215		9	Aristotle	190
3	Shakespeare	210		10	Brunelleschi	190
4	Einstein	205		11	Copernicus	185
5	Newton	195		12	Franklin	185
6	Jefferson	195		13	G.Eliot	180
7	Edison	195		14	J.S.Mill	180

There are some startling omissions from the Cox list, such as Shakespeare! There is also no excuse for leaving out Einstein, for example: his Specific and General Theories of Relativity were already well known in 1923. Our own calculations result in somewhat different conclusions on the top IQ's.

It is interesting that the Cox analysis and our totally independent enquiry both produce an identical number of IQ record holders of 180 or above. In Cox's case 14, whilst we also identified 14!

'Human Computer' Controversy

In *The Guinness Book of Records*, it is noted under the heading 'Human Computer' that the following record stands: 'The fastest extraction of a 13th root from a 100 digit number is in 1 min 28.8 sec by Willem Klein (b. 1912, Netherlands) on 7 April 1981 at the National Laboratory for High Energy Physics (KEK), Tsukuba, Japan. Mrs Shakuntal Devi of India demonstrated the multiplication of two 13-digit numbers

7,686,369,774,870 x 2,465,099,745,779

picked at random by the Computer Department of Imperial College, London on 18 June 1980, in 28 seconds. Her correct answer was 18,947,668,177,995,426,462,773,730'

The Guinness Book of Records goes on to record the extraordinary comment that: 'Some experts on calculating prodigies refuse to give credence to the above – largely on the grounds that it is so vastly superior to the calculating feats of any other invigilated prodigy.'

We respectfully point out that Mrs Devi has been invigilated a number of times, has appeared on numerous live television shows, performing 'new' calculations based on the works of various mathematics professors, and has consistently performed at the level indicated in her record-breaking performance. We support Mrs Devi in her natural excellence, and hope that researchers will increasingly realise that their amazement and amusement should lie not in the outstanding excellence of any human mental performance, but in the rarity of similar performances.

Memory Benchmarks, Past and Present

Telephone Numbers

Gon YangLing memorised just over 15,000 Chinese telephone numbers, in Harbin, China, according to the Xinhua News Agency.

Song Memorisation

Barbara 'Squeak' Moore performed 1,852 (one thousand eight hundred and fifty-two) songs from memory in Pennsylvania, USA, in 1988.

Card Speed Memory (52-card pack)

Back in 1991 Dominic O'Brien of Furneux Pelham, Herts achieved perfect memorisation in two minutes, 29 seconds on 26 October 1991 at The Athenaeum Club, London. Since 1991, this time has tumbled down, as you will discover later in the book. For now, readers may be interested to find out their own memorising ability. Memorising a pack of cards may not sound easy, but it is possible. Try with half a pack at first, and test your results against the following table:

26 cards in 30 minutes: Above average.

52 cards in 30 minutes: An excellent memory

52 cards in 15 minutes: You can out-memorise 98% of the population.

52 cards in 10 minutes: You can out-memorise 99% of the population.

52 cards in 6 minutes: Good enough to take part in national competitions

52 cards in 5 minutes: Strong national calibre

52 cards in 3 minutes: Good enough to compete in World Championships

Card Memory (inter-shuffled packs)

Dominic O'Brien on 22 July 1990 at The Star, Furneux Pelham, Herts – 35 packs (1,820 cards) in no set time limit.

Number Memorisation

Dominic O'Brien on 16 October 1991 at The Athenaeum Club, London – 266 random digits perfectly memorised forwards and backwards in 15 minutes.

Memorisation of Names and Faces

Themistocles (c.523-c.458BC) Greek soldier and statesman, was able to remember the 20,000 names of the citizens of Athens.

Xerxes, King of Persia from 486 to 465BC, was reputed to be able to recall the names of the 100,000 men in his armies.

Yet astonishingly, these figures have been dwarfed in our own time. Harry Lorayne of New York over a 'memorising lifetime' of approximately 40 years, including over 200 personal appearances a year, has memorised at least 7,500,000 names and faces! He memorised between 400 and 800 people at a time, often two to three times per day, and including numerous national television appearances. He has established a record that may never be broken.

Memorisation of Sports Facts

Frank Felberbaum of New York on 26 October 1991 at The Athenaeum Club, London – perfect memorisation of national league baseball statistics from 1876 to 1990, covering year, winning team, manager, total winning games for season, and winning percentage. Over 2,000 differing pieces of information and data.

Memorisation of Prophetic Sayings

Imam Al-Bukhari (9th century AD) memorised over 300,000 prophetic sayings (average length of about five lines) word for word. (Approximately 21,000,000 words.)

Memorisation of Holy Texts

Mr Ahand Didat memorised by heart the Holy Koran, and the Bible (Old Testament).

Memorisation of Canonical Texts

Bhanddanta Vicittabu Vumsa in May 1974 in Yangon, Myanmar (formerly Rangoon, Burma) – recited 16,000 pages of Buddhist canonical texts.

Memorisation of Tribe History

Maori Chiefs have been reported to spend as long as three days reciting the history of their tribe, passed from generation to generation.

Religious Records – Faith in Memory

Once upon a time in Poland, and in a few special areas still remaining today, the Chass Polak Jews would, as part of their regular training and everyday practice, memorise the exact position of each word on very page of the gigantic twelve volumes of the Talmud – their Bible. Similarly, in India, the entire volume of the Vedic scriptures, a work even larger than the Talmud, was passed down only by memory.

These marvellous feats of memory were considered commonplace and automatic as long as the religious student was interested in the subject, and learnt the memory principles for these scriptures appropriately. Thus memorising 'millions' of pieces of data is, historically, a natural function of an interested and well-trained brain.

Not all of the above records still stand. Some represent historical stages. As this book unfolds, you will be amazed by some of the rapid and stunning improvements!

The following item from 1991 reinforces the view that the *achievement in memory records has shot up!*

Improve your IQ by improving your Memory

In Pittsburgh, North America, an American student by the name of Dario Donatelli graduated from Carnegie-Mellon University, where he had spent his final years of study specialising in the development and practice of memory techniques.

Describing himself as a normal student, Donatelli suggests that the only difference between him and others is that he has practised appropriate techniques. In his own words: 'My memory is like anyone else's. There are probably hundreds of thousands of other people who, if they had the same interest in numbers and saw a reason to practise calculating and memory for a few years, would be faster than I am.'

Before he began his studies at university, he had shown no particular aptitude for memory of any sort, but since his study and practice of specially developed memory techniques, he has become one of the top memorisers of all-time, having broken the world record for digital memory.

That record had stood for nearly 70 years, and was set in 1911 by a German mathematics professor who memorised 18 digits, presented at just under one second per digit, without error.

Donatelli smashed this world record by remembering accurately a number of over 70 digits! The number was

151859376550157841665850611209488568677273141818610546 2974801294974965928.

Donatelli performed this prodigious memory feat by pausing for 40 seconds after the numbers had been read to him, reviewing and checking his memory technique, and then responding in the following manner: 'The first set is 1518. Then 5937...' He repeated all of the digits in order, consistently grouping them in threes or fours, as he gave the answer.

The audience observing him was obviously fascinated, and asked him to explain in more detail how he had actually done it.

He replied, 'The first set was a three-mile time, the second set was a ten-mile time, then a mile, then a half mile, then a two-mile time, then an age, then a two-mile, then a mile, then a two-mile, then two ages, then an age, then the 3,000-metre time, then a mile, then a date, then a mile, then a 10,000-metre time, then a two-mile time, then an age, then an age, then an age, and finally a two-mile time.'

In his mind's eye, Donatelli had created a fairy tale of a series of runners and people of different ages, allowing him a much easier reaccessing of what was seen by others as a totally unmemorisable number.

By improving his memory of numbers, Donatelli similarly increased his IQ score. Short-term memorisation of numbers is one of the major factors in determining your IQ. The average person can remember between six and seven digits presented at the standard rate of just under a second. This would give an IQ of 100 in this sub-area of overall IQ. A score of eight correct would leap you to between 120 and 130 IQ. And a score of nine to ten would rank you in the genius 140+ IQ range.

Thus, Donatelli has developed this particular aspect of his own intelligence to an IQ level so high that it is immeasurable. You can do the same!

CHAPTER TWO

MEMORY RECORDS

A Brief History of Memory

Who would have thought it? Over three thousand years later and Homer's *The Iliad* is a hot topic of news. With the launch of the film *Troy* starring Brad Pitt, controversy was raging as to the authenticity of the story line. *The Telegraph* Newspaper chose to use its leader column to make the bold statement that Brad Pitt was just as qualified to given an impression of what actually occurred as any Regis Professor of Greek. They base this surprising statement on the fact that *The Iliad* was originally created as a spoken story some five hundred years after The Trojan War happened. It was then passed down from Bard to Bard for some seven hundred more years before anyone thought to write it down. On this basis, they argue, it is hard to accept any of the events described as historically accurate.

But is that a fair assumption? It is certainly true that, by today's standards, such a feat as memorising the entire *Iliad* would be highly exceptional. But is that because we have so many other ways of capturing and retaining knowledge that we no longer need to cultivate this in built talent?

With computers getting so small that they can fit in the palm of your hand, and with the facility now to access the entire contents of the internet through the air and without any physical connection, why bother trying to memorise anything when you can locate that information in seconds.

They say that the factories of the future will be completely managed by one man and a dog. The man will be there to look after the dog, and the dog will be there to make sure that the man doesn't touch the machines. Could it be that we are starting to rely too much on those machines? Are we witnessing a dumbing down of mental skills past a point of no return? With memory, is it a question of 'Use it or Lose it'?

Taking a look back at history, the art of memory goes back a long way. In early oral traditions, the poet was the most important member of the community since they knew all of the words, and the stories which the words made. They know the order in which society existed. In pre-Christian Ireland the poet was in a social status right next to the king. In battle, kings could be killed, the killing of a poet was considered to be the worst sacrilege. Poets of opposing armies would often begin a battle by flinging satires at each other.

This oral tradition required the development of memory without using written systems. Stories had to be learnt and recited with complete and unfailing accuracy, with no room for variations. This required a long and rigorous apprenticeship. As a result, stories varied little over long periods of time and were well-known by everyone within the society.

In Australia, the indigenous people maintained a 40,000 year old culture through songs. Every rock and crack has a song associated with it and the whole continent can be sung like a musical score. In this way, stories have been faithfully passed down from generation to generation, without the need to write.

This oral tradition can be found in every continent from the tribes of Africa to the tradition of the seanachie in Scotland. So for the Telegraph to suggest that this ancient and noble art of memory was not up to the job in accurately passing down Homer's *Iliad* for a few short centuries, is just not true.

The Art of Memory

The Art of Memory has been discovered afresh many times over the centuries as different people have discovered how amazing the human brain really is.

The ancient Greek Poet Simonides of Ceos was said to have invented the Art of Memory. The legend has it that he was invited to recite verses at a banquet. As was the fashion in those times, he started with a few lines in honour of the gods. In this case he praised Castor and Pollux before settling down to the serious business of praising his host. Less than pleased by this, his host only paid him half of his fee and suggested that he obtain the rest from the deities he had praised.

Shortly after, a servant came up to Simonides and told him that there were two men on horseback at the door asking for him. The poet went outside but found nobody there. At that moment the roof of the banquet hall collapsed behind him killing his host and all the other guests. It appeared that Castor and Pollux, traditionally pictured as two young horsemen, had indeed paid their half of the fee.

However, the story had an unexpected twist. When the bodies of the dead were later recovered, they were so badly mangled that even their relations could not identify them. Simonides found that, by mentally picturing the hall he was able to remember the order that the guests had been sitting and, as a result, was able to identify the dead. As he later pondered on this ability, he realised that the technique that he had used could be the key to Art of Memory.

Using this concept, orators could picture the hall in which there were to speak and allocate the subject matter to particular architectural features to help them to memorise them. This technique is still used today. In later centuries, this idea also gave rise to the concept of a Memory Palace.

During the Middle Ages memory techniques once again came into fashion and practicing the Art of Memory was seen as an act of Prudence, one of the seven Cardinal Virtues. Later still during the Renaissance, it became a common accomplishment of the educated. In the hands of practitioners like Giordano Bruno the traditional methods of memorising gave rise to new and intricate systems. Even the arrival of printing and cheap and plentiful paper barely cut into its popularity and it was only with the coming of the 17th century and the Scientific Revolution that it finally fell into obscurity

So, as oral traditions gave way to written ones, and as parchment gave way to book and books gave way to computers, so the need for the brain to retain vast quantities of knowledge has diminished and so the Art of Memory fell out of general favour, kept alive by a only by a small band of enthusiasts.

A History of the Memoriads

The First Memoriad

But, in the final decade of the last Millennium something happened which turned the sport around. Tony Buzan, Raymond Keene and Vanda North created the framework for a competition of ten different memory disciplines and staged the very first World Memory Championship which took place in London's Athenæum on the 26 October 1991 under the title of Memoriad '91. Sponsored by Buzan Centres this event attracted international media attention and has been the springboard to a resurgence of interest.

Since then memory competitions have grabbed headlines and the public's imagination with ordinary people, from all walks of life, performing seemingly impossible mental feats. The professions represented by the competitors to this first competition included Banker, Telephone Operator, Student of English, Psychiatric Nurse, Operations Manager of a cleaning company at Stansted Airport, a Business Consultant and a Computer Operator. In today's competitions it is even more diverse.

The 1991 event attracted the top memorisers of the day and included:

- Bruce Balmer, who had learnt 2,000 foreign words in one day (18 hours)
- Philip Bond, holder of the then World Number Memory Record at 236 random numbers memorised in 30 minutes.
- Creighton Carvello, who memorised the number Pi to 20,013 places
- Jonathon Hancock, 1988 World Record Holder for memorising

six packs of cards, and student at Christchurch, Oxford

- Harry Lorayne, the doyen of American memory masters and the 'elder statesman' of world memory experts

- Dominic O'Brien, Guinness Book of World Records holder for consecutive card park memory (35!)

- Nwodo Ohaka, the 'telecom memory man' known as the 'organic computer' for his ability to memorise 6,755 U.K. telephone dialing codes

- Kenneth Wilshire, mental athlete whose memory is so good it allows him to play Casino Blackjack successfully.

Needless to say with such diverse and colourful competitors, the 1991 event was a suspense- filled affair, with world records smashed along the way, and the overall Championship being decided with the last competition.

After the first three of seven events, Memorisation of Names and Faces, Numbers, and Random Words, the two favourites, Creighton Carvello and Dominic O'Brien, were lying third and first respectively, with the young outsider, Jonathon Hancock, being a surprising second, having won two of the events, but having done poorly in the Memorisation of Random Numbers.

In this event, in which the competitors were given 15 minutes to memorise a thousand-digit number, Dominic O'Brien came first, smashing Philip Bond's previous record with the perfect memorisation of 266 numbers, backwards and forwards, in fifteen minutes.

In the next three competitions, the Memorisation of Chess Positions, Written Text, and Chinese Vocabulary, O'Brien and Hancock increased the tension, battling it out for first place in each competition, O'Brien winning Chess and Chinese memorisation, Hancock Text.

Thus, going into the final event, the Speed Memorisation of a shuffled pack of 52 cards, both O'Brien and Hancock had won three competitions each, while Carvello posed a constant threat.

This was particularly true in the final competition, where Carvello held the world record for the memorisation of a pack of cards at 2 minutes 59 seconds with only one error.

On this last competition rested. the overall championship; Carvello's world record; and the reputation of at least four of the competitors who had publicly stated that they felt they could beat Carvello's bench-mark!

The cards were shuffled by David Berglas, President of the Inner Circle of Magicians. Each competitor was handed a pack of cards by his own personal adjudicator, and the mental combat began. The task was to memorise, in order, the pack of cards, and when having done so immediately to hand the cards to the adjudicator while raising the hand. Thus the competitor had not only to memorise the entire pack perfectly (in the competition no errors were allowed) but had to know when the memorisation was complete.

After 2 minutes and 29 seconds, Dominic O'Brien's hand shot up as he handed his pack to the adjudicator. He then buried his head in his hands. Carvello finished in just under 4 minutes, and the remaining competitors took the maximum of 5. As the adjudicators walked away with the competitors, no one knew whether O'Brien had misjudged his memory, whether Carvello had indeed memorised perfectly and therefore maintained his number one ranking, or whether the more cautious competitors had been justifiably so.

After ten minutes of adjudication, all the results were in with the exception of Dominic O'Brien, and Jonathon Hancock was well ahead of the field with 46 cards perfectly memorised in order before making an error. Carvello had slipped up on an early card.

All then rested on the return of the final adjudicator: the World Championship, the World Speed Card Memory Record, and the individual winner of the final event. Raymond Keene, O.B.E., Dominic O'Brien's adjudicator, finally marched in with the comment 'Perfect!' In what was the equivalent to the Shoot-Out at the OK. Corral and to High Noon, Dominic O'Brien had convincingly and brilliantly won the first World Memory Championships, breaking two world records in the process, and becoming a 'Brain Star' overnight. His first words after having been announced the winner and being asked by NBC what his reactions were to being the first World Memory Champion were 'To win it again next year!'.

The Growth of the Memoriad

Since this first World Championship the event has been held almost every year since then with the number of participants and the countries they represent, growing each time. For the first decade of the tournament Dominic O'Brien dominated the event winning it every year, with the exception of 1994 when he came second to Jonathan Hancock and 1998, when he was unable to compete and the title was won by Andi Bell. In the 2002 event, Andi was determined to prove the validity of his first win, and went head to head with Dominic for the title. In a breathtaking and inspired final Andi achieved an overall score of 6,927, 566 points ahead of his rival, and smashing all previous records to take the title. This achievement is equivalent to when the international chess grandmaster and world champion Bobby

Fischer broke the 'impossible' 2,700 barrier in chess.

Prior to this championship, only Dominic O'Brien had ever achieved over 6,000 championship points with Dr Gunther Karsten of Germany being the only other person to achieve over 5,000.

The Millennium Standard

The scoring system used in the Championships is based on The Millennium Standard. This is calculated by averaging the current world records and adding 10% to 15%, to create a maximum available points of 1,000 per competition and 10,000 overall. A fuller explanation can be found on the World Memory Championship website – www.worldmemorychampionships.com

Each year the World Memory Championships pushes away at the boundaries of what seems to be possible, proving time and time again that we seriously underestimate the capacity of the brain.

Through his books on the subject, Tony Buzan has probably generated more interest in the sport than anyone else and has worked tirelessly as an international ambassador for memory, inspiring educationalists, governments and businesses, to wake up to the amazing potential of the human brain.

People often ask the question, 'What's point of memorizing giant lists of words and numbers. Isn't it just a waste of time?' The answer is a resounding 'No!'. In the same way that you don't criticise people in a gym for using a rowing machine and not going anywhere, so also must you treat the brain just like a muscle and give it exercise in the same way.

The more you train your memory, the more you train your creativity. The more you train you creativity, the more you train your memory.

The Mind Sport of Memory took a major step towards it being recognised at an important discipline in its own right, with the formation of the World Memory Sports Council. Endorsed by leading memorisers across the world, the WMSC has built on the pioneering world by Tony Buzan, Raymond Keene and Vanda North and formalised a structure for memory competitions at all levels. Supported with a Code of Ethics for the Sport, and the Rules and Regulations for each discipline, this has created a level playing field and made possible international competition and the World Memory Championships to take place.

The website of the WMSC, www.worldmemorychampionships.com contains the records of every World Championships since 1991 and publishes the World Rankings of the sport. The WMSC also supports the World Memory Sports Club which includes a discussion forum on its website for memorisors around the world to share ideas and information.

The 2003 World Memory Championships (Kuala Lumpur)

For people whose experience of sport is limited to watching an inflated leather balloon getting kicked or thrown around an oblong of grass, it must be difficult to comprehend the fact that watching mental sports can have the same level of excitement and tension. However, the World Memory Championships, which took place in Malaysia in October 2003, generated as much if not more.

In the thirteenth year of competition, 2003 was the first time that the event had been held outside the UK. Hosted on behalf of the World Memory Sports Council by Maximum Recall in Kuala Lumpur, a record number of 55 competitors from 20 countries competed for the prize of being recognised as the World Memory Champion. The results were surprising and dramatic.

Whilst previous competitions have seen an increasing number of women competitors the sport, up till now, has been dominated by men. Year after year, Dominic O'Brien, the eight times World Champion, has fought off competition primarily from Andi Bell, the 2002 winner. This year was to be very different with the largest ever number of women competitors taking part and the undisputed rise of the female mnemonist.

Malaysia proved to be an excellent host country for the event which was recognised at the highest level both by the Government of Malaysia and also with the attendance of Royalty at the final awards dinner.

For those new to the sport, the competition is divided into ten separate disciplines, which take place over a three-day period. Strict WMSC rules govern the event and independent arbiters supervise individual competitors. This years' event was under the personal supervision of the WMSC Chief Arbiter, Phil Chambers, and the previous year's WMC Chief Arbiter, Jennifer Goddard.

Day one of the competition opened with the first discipline, the Poem, an event that augured the rise of the female! Astrid Plessl shot into the lead with a world record performance of 345 which also hit the Millennium Standard for the event. Two other female competitors, both Juniors, Christiane Stenger and Ivy Chong See Mun, took second and third places with MSO champion Ben Pridmore in fourth.

The second event was Binary Digits in which the men fought back with Gunther Karsten, Ben Pridmore and Jan Formann taking the top three places with Andi Bell and Dominic O'Brien in fourth and fifth. Although Astrid was seventh place in this discipline, her stunning opening score ensured that she held on to her first place in the championship with Ben and Gunther now in second and third.

With the pace now hotting up, the third discipline was One Hour Cards. Here, astonishingly, the top twenty two competitors all achieved the Grand Master Norm with the top four being Andi Bell, Jan Formann, Ben Pridmore and Dominic O'Brien. Astrid Plessl was fifth but still managed to hold onto her overall lead in the championships. Christiane Stenger, a junior, was still in the top ten overall at number seven. Two female competitors in the top ten had not occurred before in the history of Mind Sports – could the ladies maintain this unprecedented accomplishment?.

Discipline four was Names and Faces in which competitors are presented with sheets of photographs to memorise. This time Andi Bell took first place with Astrid second and the reining American Champion, Scott Hagwood, in third. However, Astrid still held onto her overall championships lead for the fourth discipline in a row. With Christiane Stenger holding seventh place overall, there were still two females in the top ten. Would it continue?

Speed Numbers were discipline number five and Jan Formann achieved a new world record with 324 to take first place followed by another leading female competitor, Christina Brunger, memorising an impressive 288 numbers in five minutes and Ginther Karsten in third with 280. However there were now *three* females in the top ten. Astrid Plessl had still held onto her first place with total championship points of 3596, with Andi Bell on 3364 and Ben Pridmore on 3281. Also in the top ten were Christiane Stenger and Christina Brunger.

The final discipline on day two of the championships was Historic Dates, and historic this event turned out to be. Ben Pridmore achieved an amazing new World Record with a raw event score of 60. Gunther Karsten, Andi Bell and Astrid Plessl were second, third and forth. Ben's record score now catapulted him to first place in the championship so far, and pushed Astrid Plessl into second place overall.

However, all this activity at the top shouldn't distract from other amazing performances elsewhere. A sixteen year old Malaysian girl, Ivy Chong See Mun competing for the first time, hit the Grand Master Norm in this discipline, an amazing achievment.

So day two ended with much excitement, new records and the possibility of some real surprises ahead. Who says that mind sports don't have the same appeal as physical sports? Looking at the competitors as they left to freshen up and rest, you could see how physically exhausting the day had been for them. Memorising is harder work than you might realise. With only a mere 500 points separating the 1st and 5th places there was still everything to play for.

Day three started with a magnificent Malaysian dawn but for the competitors it was only a brief glance before it was back to work for another full day of stiff competition.

The first discipline of the day, and the seventh in the competition, was the One Hour Number. And with my now familiar call of "Dendrites at the ready, go!" it was eyes down once again. One hour later, and there were more surprises. This time it was the turn of Jan Formann to have the limelight with a new world record. Jan takes the sport very seriously, but not himself. He is one of Germany's top clowns and comedians. But with competition really starting to hot up, no one was laughing now. In the one-hour cards Andi Bell, Gunther Karsten, Ben Pridmore and now Christina Braunger were in 2nd to 5th positions. Ben Pridmore hung onto his competition lead with Andi Bell in second place and the day one and two star, Astrid Plessl now in overall third.

Next discipline was Random Words and it was all change yet again. This time Astrid Plessl stormed back to first place and also first place in the championship. Having been in the dominant position in six of the disciplines so far and second in one other, she was obviously a force to be reckoned with. But could she shake off her challengers in the remaining two disciplines? Random Words saw Dominic O'Brien in second place, followed by Gunther

Karsten and Andi Bell. Would they stand by and see a historic first win from a female competitor? Things were getting serious.

Spoken Number was next and a hush fell on the room once again as the each number was read out at precisely one second intervals. This time it was Andi Bell and Gunther Karsten in the top two places both with World Record scores. Astrid Plessl came third but remained number one in the overall competition. Could she make it through one more discipline and claim the title? Still in the top ten was junior, Christine Stenger and Christina Braunger was just outside at number eleven. But what would happen next?

By this time the atmosphere was electric. Speed Cards is one of the most dramatic discplines. It is fast and exciting to watch. It also requires maximum concentration and nerves of steel. With so much still to play for it would test the competitors to the maximum. It is also a test of mathematics as the leaders weigh up the number of points they need and decide whether to go all out for speed and risk missing a card or to go for safety and lose a precious second or two. Tough call. Minutes later and it was all over. The arbitors left to work out the score leaving everyone on tenderhooks.

It was going to be close.

In the end out of a winning score of 6701 there were just 28 points between the winner and the runner up: a percentage of 0.41%! And the winner? Andi Bell, with Astrid Plessl in second place, Ben Pridmore – third, Gunther Karsten – 4th, Jan Formann – 5th and Dominic O'Brien in 6th. There were only 944 points separating the top six.

For the first time since the start of the championships in 1992, two female competitors ended up in the top ten. Christina Braunger was 11th and with Ivy Chong See Mun finishing at 15th, two junior girls were in the top twenty.

Five new World Records were achieved in the championships. The first was in the poem. This record had stood since 1995 when Patrick Colgan achieved a score of 260. Since then no one has come close. This year Astrid Plessl claimed it for here own with an amazing score of 345. A new world record and a shattering of the Millennium Standard.

In Speed Numbers and Hour Numbers Jan Formann broke both World Records. Ben Pridmore the MSO Champion, smashed the Historic Dates record of 51 with a score of 60. And in the Spoken Numbers discipline both Andi Bell and Gunther Karsten smashed Dominic O'Briens 2001 record of 128 with scores of 140 and 131 respectively. And this in a discipline that a University of London psychologist said some years ago that no one in the world would ever remember more than 30!

In the achievement of Grand Master Norms, 16 year old Malaysian girl Ivy

Chong See Mun, competing as a Junior, in the Hour Number required a score of 721 but achieved 758. In the One hour Cards, she needed to memorise seven packs but acutually achieved nine. In Speed cards she needed to achieve three minutes but instead did it in 1.25! She is certainly a name to watch for in the future.

The reigning American Champion, Scott Hagwood, who continues to dominate the sport in the USA despite having undergone heavy radio therapy for cancer which potentially could have impaired his memory, smashed the American record in both Hour Number and Speed Cards and achieved the Grand Master Norm. He is the first American Grand Master and a wonderful ambassador for the sport.

Finishing the event as 20th in the world was another Junior Yudi Lesmana from Indonesia who came 6th in the Speed Cards and is the first Indonesian Grand Master.

The first competitor from China to achieve Grand Master was MaoHua Wang who achieved a championships score of 1748 and is rated 29th in the world.

In fact the individual achievements of all competitors was nothing short of amazing and although attention is inevitably drawn to the top of the leader board in such an event, every competitor deserves warm congratulations.

The 2004 World Memory Championships (Manchester)

The first day of competition in the 2004 World Memory Championships has proved, once again, that you can never underestimate the power and capacity of the human brain.

The 2004 event saw twenty three competitors from nine countries participating which included Austria, England, Germany, France, Singapore, South Africa, USA, Norway and Sweden. The competitors from China sadly missed the event due to visa difficulties.

Three times World Champion and Grand Master of Memory Andi Bell was present to defend his WMSC title. Determined to relieve him of it was the 2003 Silver Medalist and top seed, Astrid Plessl of Austria with Ben Pridmore of England, Dr Guther Karsten of Germany, and a host of others with similar intent.

The first two events of the day, the memorising of a previously unpublished, non-rhyming poem and the memorising of binary digits produced a foretaste of what will be in store over the remaining two days of competition.

The first surprise of the day was not long in coming. Two juniors were in the top four places. Joachim Thaler and Corinna Drashci, both from Austria.

Joachim beat the entire field to achieve the Millennium Standard, the silver medal and a score of 310.5. Gold Medal went to the cool Astrid Plessl who, sitting quietly at the back of the room, achieved 312 points and the Millennium Standard.

The second event of the day, Binary Digits, proved to be even more surprising. With sheets of ones and zeros to memorise, the event is a real challenge both for competitors and also the arbiters marking the sheets.

After 30 minutes of memorisation and one hour for recall the scores were marked over lunch.

In the top five, junior competitor Joachim was still holding his own in fifth place (and third in the championship) with a score of 2106. Andi Bell was moving up with 2553 and Astrid had 2715. However, the world record had been smashed by Dr Gunther Karsten with an impressive score of 3384. But even with that he could only manage a silver medal. With a truly amazing score of 3705, Ben Pridmore had left the entire field standing with a new, new world record. Things were indeed hotting up.

The final event of the day – One Hour Card memorisation started mid afternoon with the faint sounds of Manchester's Gay Pride March filtering through the circular windows of the Barns Wallace Building of UMIST. With some competitors asking for over thirty packs of cards to memorise, the arbiters resigned themselves to working late into the night to count the results. Thirteen competitors achieved their GM Norms including a new Grand Master Luise Sommer who qualified on the day.

In the second event running, England's Ben Pridmore was in gold medal position with 1144 cards, 22 packs correctly memorised. Silver went to Astrid Plessl with 18.6 packs. Bronze was Steffen Buetow with 16 packs.

Sunday, the second day of competition produced a morning of dramatic developments. Firstly a resurgent Andi Bell smashed his own world record of 156 in the Names and Faces discipline achieving an impressive score of 167.5.

The leader at the close of Saturday's competition, Ben Pridmore, who himself had smashed the Binary Digits record with an incredible 3705 faltered in the Names and Faces discipline coming twelfth with a score of 79.

Astrid Plessl, who finished Saturday in second place to Ben, herself a world record holder in the Poem discipline, fared better, closely tracking Andi Bell and coming second in Names and Faces, with a score of 145.5

The result of this incredibly tense and exceptionally competitive first event of the second day was that Astrid moved up into first position with Ben second and Andi in third. Sixteen year-old Joachim Thaler, was still more than holding his own with a score of 136.5.

Event Five was the Speed Number in which competitors have two attempts to memorise as many digits as possible in five minutes. The current world record is held by Jan Formann with 324. At the half way point of the competition the top five in this discipline included, in joint fifth position, Gunther Karsten and Joachim Thaler with 224. Fourth was Lukas Amsuess with 252.

In Bronze position Andi Bell had 256, and in Silver was Ben Pridmore with 302. Scoring yet another victory was Astrid Plessl with 302.

At this half way point, the battle for the gold medal was incredibly close: with 4028 championship points, Astrid on 126 points ahead of Ben Pridmore with 3902 and 578 points ahead of third place Andi with 3450.

Astrid was poised to become the first ever female Mind Sports Champion in history. Both Astrid and Ben also on course for being the first Grand Masters to break the magic 7,000 point barrier in competition.

Another point of interest is that the current top ten includes three female competitors – the first time in the history of mind sports that this has occurred. The three are: Astrid Plessl, the current leader, a twenty year old medical student; Alisa Kellner, an eighteen year old student, and Luise Sommer a 49 year old teacher and author.

The World Country Championships are also hotting up: England, the pre tournament top seed, with a score of 9,584, rose from last nights third position, to second, overtaking Germany, who are now in third with 8,675 points. The leaders remain Austria with an impressive score of 10,037.

The final day of competition, Monday saw the climax of the competition with Random Words, Spoken Number and finally the dramatic Speed Card Competition in which the competitors have to attempt to remember perfectly, in less than a minute, an entire deck of fifty two playing cards.

After an intense day, the final results were announced with a new champion, Ben Pridmore winning the 2004 World Memory Championships

The three days of competition saw the unattainable barrier of seven thousand points totally smashed, there were five world records broken – two of them twice, and a Junior, winning championship Bronze. An amazing event.

Ben Pridmore won with 8,302 points. Astrid Plessl last year's Sliver Medalist won Silver again but this time with 7,508 points. Sixteen year old Joachim Thaler from Austria had a tremendous competition and won Bronze with 6,367.

There were World Records broken in Binary Digits, Names and Faces, Historic Dates, Random Words and speed Cards in the highest scoring competition ever. The average age of competitors this year was 25.

The Final Top Ten

Ben Pridmore GM (Eng) 8,302

Astrid Plessl (Aus – age 20) 7,508

Joachim Thaler (Aus) JNR 6,367

Clemens Mayer (Ger) 6,253

Alisa Kellner (Ger) JNR 5,793

Boris Konrad (Ger) 5,778

Andi Bell (UK) 5,767

Gunter Karsten (Ger) 5,729

Lukas Amsuess (Aus) 5,602

Luise Sommer (Aus) 4,789

Memory Record holders

Current Adult Record holders – for men and women aged 18-59

Event	Name	Result
One Hour Numbers	Jan Formann	1920
Speed Numbers	Jan Formann	324
Binary Numbers	Ben Pridmore	3705
Spoken Numbers	Andi Bell	140
One Hour Cards	Andi Bell	1197
Speed Cards	Andi Bell	32.9
Names and Faces	Andi Bell	167.5
Poem	Astrid Plessl	345
Random Words	Joachim Thaler	189
Historic Dates	Ben Pridmore	80

Junior World Record Holders – for students 13 – 17

Event	Name	Result
One Hour Numbers	Yu Zhang	1560
Speed Numbers	Yu Zhang	314
Binary Numbers	Yu Zhang	2745
Spoken Numbers	Christiane Stenger	79
One Hour Cards	Yu Zhang	1040
Speed Cards	Chan Tian How	76.53
Names and Faces	Sebastian Bunk	107
Poem	Christiane Stenger	139
Random Words	Joachim Thaler	189
Historic Dates	Sebastian Bunk	56

Children World Record Holders – for children 12 or younger

Event	Name	Result
One Hour Numbers	Christiane Stenger	732
Speed Numbers	Katharina Bunk	145
Binary Numbers	Christiane Stenger	795
Spoken Numbers	Katharina Bunk	36
One Hour Cards	Christiane Stenger	368
Speed Cards	Katharina Bunk	74.5
Names and Faces	Katharina Bunk	90
Poem	Lara Hick	122
Random Words	Katharina Bunk	90
Historic Dates	Sebastian Bunk	38

Grandmaster of Memory

The title of Grand Master of Memory was first awarded in October 1995 at a Memory Awards Ceremony in Hanbury Manor. The event was a conscious homage to the very first award of chess grandmaster titles at St Petersburg in 1914 by Czar Nicholas 11 to the greats of the world's most widespread mind sport. The original chess grandmasters were Emanuel Lasker, José Raoul Capablanca, Alexander Alekhine, Siegbert Tarrasch and Frank Marshall. The award of the memory titles was jointly sanctioned by His Serene Highness Prince Philip von und zu Liechtenstein, The Brain Trust Charity, which endorsed and hosted the event, and Tony Buzan, International Arbiter of Mental World Records.

At the time of publishing, there were thirty four Grand Master of Memory: Andi Bell, Astrid Plessl, Ben Pridmore, Christiane Stenger, Christina Braunger, David Thomas, Dominic O'Brien, Dr M Buchvaldová, Gunther Karsten, Fanny Boediman, How Chan Tian, Ivy Chong See Mun (J), Jan Formann, John Louis, Jonathan Hancock, Katharina Bunk, Kevin Horsley, Lukas Amsüss, MaoHua Wang, Michael Tipper, Nishant Kasibhatla, Patrick Colgan, Prapti Hartiningsih, Robert Carder, Scott Hagwood, Steffen Bütow, Stephen Clarke, Swe Chooi Yip, Titiani Loren, Wan Jiun Wong, Wiwik Setyowati, Yuan Ooi Shyong, Yudi Lesmana (J), Zhang Jie

To join their ranks you need to be able to memorise 1000 digits in an hour, ten randomly shuffled decks of cards in one hour, and be able to memorise one deck of cards in two minutes. The qualification for Grand Master is to achieve a minimum of 6,000 points in the ten disciplines of a memory competition. The disciplines are Spoken Number, Poem, Binary Digits, hour Cards, Names and Faces, speed number, Historic/Future dates, One Hour Numbers, Random words and speed Cards. Full details of the rules of memory competitions can be found on www.worldmemorychampionship.com.

The WMSC Millennium Standard Counting System for the World Memory Championships was inspired by the standard points systems used in the World and Olympic track-and-field event, the Decathlon (a similar scoring system is used for the Pentathlon and Heptathlon).

In the Decathlon, the International Athletic Committees set Future Standards in each event, which were comfortably above the world records in that event. They were set as future goals, and as 'Future Standards' against which any Decathlete could measure current performance, current world standing, and future goals. If an athlete were to reach the Future Standard in any of the 10 events, that athlete would receive 1,000 points for that event.

Thus an 'ideal' performance would be to smash the World Records in each of the 10 events, and in the process reaching the 'Future Standard' goal. Such a performance would give the competitor a perfect 10,000 points. It is interesting to note that in the Decathlon for many decades the '9,000 barrier' was never broken. Only recently has this happened, with the Czech champion holding the current record of 9,026 Decathlon points.

The WMSC Millennium Standard Counting System is based on the same principles. For each of the 10 memory events, a new Millennium Standard 1,000-point goal has been established.

This 1,000-point goal has been calculated taking into consideration the following factors:

1. The actual current World Record.
2. The rate of increase/progression of that world record over the last 10 years.
3. The results in the particular competition of Grandmasters in National and World Competitions over the last 10 years.
4. Stated results of Grandmasters and Championship competitors during practice.

The WMSC Millennium Standard is on average between 10-15% more than the current World Record, and is seen as a goal that should be reachable within the next 2-5 years by the best in the world at any particular discipline.

As an example: in the 1-hour Numbers, the actual World Record is 1,820 digits perfectly memorized. The Millennium Standard (the 1,000-point goal) is set out at 2,500 digits perfectly memorized. The current World Record, 1,820, is 72.8% of the 2,500 goal. Thus the Millennium Standard Counting System yields a score of 728 for a World Record performance.

The World's Top 100 Memorisers

	Name	m/f	Nat.	Comp.	Date	Pts.
1	Pridmore, Ben <u>WMC</u> (IGM)	m	GB	World	28-30.8.04	8302
2	Plessl, Astrid[1.] (IGM)	f	A	World	28-30.8.04	7508
3	Mayer, Clemens ·(IGM)	m	GER	National	21.11.04	7074
4	Bell, Andi (IGM)	m	GB	World	24-26.8.02	6927
5	Karsten Dr., Gun-	m	GER	Internat.	4/5.7.03	6557
6	Thaler, Joachim [1.J] ('87) (IGM)	m	A	World	28-30.8.04	6367
7	O´Brien, Dominic (IGM)	m	GB	World	24-26.8.02	6361
8	Formann, Jan (IGM)	m	DK	World	3-5.10.03	6061
9	Kellner, Alisa (IM)	f	GER	World	28-30.8.04	5793
10	Konrad, Boris-Nikolai (IM)	m	GER	World	28-30.8.04	5778
11	Amsüss, Lukas (GM³)	m	A	World	28-30.8.04	5602
12	Cooke, Edward (IM³)	m	GB	National	21.11.04	5490
13	Yip Dr., Swe Chooi (GM³)	m	MAL	World	24-26.8.02	5322
14	Sommer, Luise-Maria (IM)	f	A	National	23.11.03	4970
15	Zhang, Yu [J] (IM)	m	USA	World †	26/27.8.99	4805
16	Stenger, Christiane (GM³)	f	GER	World	3-5.10.03	4795
17	Bütow, Steffen (GM³)	m	GER	Internat.	4/5.7.03	4710
18	Bunk, Katharina [K] ('91) (IM)	f	GER	National	23.11.03	4681
19	Bunk, Sebastian [J] ('88) (IM)	m	GER	National	23.11.03	4577
20	Kasibhatla, Nishant [1.] (GM³)	m	IND	World	3-5.10.03	4514
21	How, Chan Tian (GM³)	m	MAL	World	25/26.8.01	4483
22	Kappus, Gaby (IM)	w	GER	World	28-30.8.04	4386
23	Carder, Robert (GM³)	m	GB	World	24-26.8.02	4216
24	Hancock, Jonathan (GM³)	m	GB	World †	5/6.8.95	4210
25	Braunger, Christina (GM³)	f	GER	Internat.	4/5.7.03	4182
26	Wiese, Katrin	f	GER	Internat.	30/31.7.04	3991
27	Mallow, Johannes	m	GER	Internat.	30/31.7.04	3987

	Name	m/f	Nat.	Comp.	Date	Pts.
28	Buchvaldová Dr., M. [1.]	f	CZ	World	24-26.8.02	3977
29	Mandl, Giselher	m	GER	Internat.	30/31.7.04	3932
30	Yuan, Ooi Shyong [J] (GM[3])	m	MAL	World	25/26.8.01	3889
31	Thomas, David (GM[3])	m	GB	World †	22/23.8.97	3657
32	Feuchter, Loredana (IM)	f	RO	National	23.11.03	3647
33	Corney, Daniel	m	GB	World †	21/22.8.00	3644
34	Draschl, Corinna [J]	f	A	World	28-30.8.04	3600
35	Stoll, Maurice	m	USA	World	28-30.8.04	3511
36	Hagwood, Scott [1.]	m	USA	World	3-5.10.03	3475
37	Harms, Jan	m	GER	Internat.	4/5.7.03	3432
38	Rydzikowski, Roman	m	GER	Internat.	30/31.7.04	3430
39	Schumeckers, Franz-Josef	m	GER	Internat.	4/5.7.03	3423
40	Turecek, Katja	f	A	National	24.11.01	3410
41	Smauley, Mike	m	GER	Internat.	30/31.7.04	3410
42	Ali, Tansel	m	AUS	World	3-5.10.03	3369
43	Clarke, Stephen (GM[3])	m	GB	World †	26/27.8.99	3348
44	Becker, David	m	SA	World	24-26.8.02	3348
45	Walk, Nathan [1.J]	m	AUS	National	10.7.04	3299
46	Röschel, Bernhard [J]	m	A	World	3-5.10.03	3276
47	Ivy, Chong See Mun [J]	f	MAL	World	3-5.10.03	3239
48	Louis, John (GM[3])	m	IND	World	3-5.10.03	3222
49	Wan, Jiun Wong (GM[3])	m	MAL	World	3-5.10.03	3214
50	Hick, Lara [K ('92)]	f	GER	World	28-30.8.04	3151
51	Orton, Simon [1.]	m	AUS	National	10.7.04	3146
52	Horsley, Kevin (GM[3])	m	SA	World	3-5.10.03	3081
53	Trevor, Nell	m	SA	World	28-30.8.04	3075
54	Hartiningsih, Prapti	f	RI	World	3-5.10.03	3058
55	Colgan, Patrick (GM[3])	m	IRL	World †	5/6.8.95	3055

	Name	m/f	Nat.	Comp.	Date	Pts.
56	Teutsch, Thomas	m	GER	Internat.	30/31.7.04	3047
57	Lesmana, Yudi J ('88) (GM³)	f	RI	World	3-5.10.03	3044
58	Anwar, Adel	m	GB	World †	26/27.08.99	3021
59	Schmitt, Christian	m	GER	Internat.	30/31.7.04	2992
60	Galinski, Marlo	m	GER	Regional	4.7.04	2851
61	Petersen, Jürgen	m	GER	Internat.	30/31.7.04	2839
62	Low, Michelle	f	SGP	World	28-30.8.04	2822
63	Dellé, Florian	m	GER	World	28-30.8.04	2795
64	Oddbjorn, Vegard	m	N	World	28-30.8.04	2778
65	Parmar, Coral	m	USA	World †	26/27.8.99	2766
66	Old, Graham	m	GB	World †	21/22.8.00	2712
67	Groves, Tom	m	GB	World †	21/22.8.00	2660
68	Görlitz, Gerhard	m	GER	Internat.	30/31.7.04	2610
69	Tipper, Michael (GM³)	m	GB	World †	27/28.8.98	2598
70	Bauer, Russell	m	AUS	National	5.10.02	2531
71	Zainuddin, Mohd. Helmi	m	MAL	World	3-5.10.03	2525
72	Setyowati, Wiwik (GM³)	f	RI	World	3-5.10.03	2522
73	Hassan, Metin	m	AUS	National	10.7.04	2519
74	Mayer-Lauingen, Martina	w	GER	Internat.	30/31.7.04	2515
75	Mar, Poh Yien J	m	Mal	World †	21/22.8.00	2474
76	Teck Hoe, Lim	m	MAL	World	24-26.8.02	2463
77	Smith, Darren	m	GB	World	25/26.8.01	2448
78	Jie, Zhang (GM³)	m	RC	World	3-5.10.03	2448
79	Pillas, Demitris	m	CY	World	25/26.8.01	2435
80	Forde, Chris	m	GB	World	25/26.8.01	2418
81	Izzati, Nur J	f	MAL	World	3-5.10.03	2413
82	Channon, Mark	m	GB	World †	5/6.8.95	2389
83	Loren, Titiani	f	RI	World	25/26.8.01	2323

	Name	m/f	Nat.	Comp.	Date	Pts.
84	Pidor, Mykie	m	USA	World	25/26.8.01	2261
85	Pötsch, Walter	m	A	National	23.11.03	2237
86	Rytířová, Michaela	f	CZ	National	1.7.01	2228
87	Yeo, Xue Ying	f	SGP	World	28-30.8.04	2209
88	Mee Keng, Lim	m	Mal	World †	21/22.8.00	2187
89	Pinnecke, Stefanie	f	GER	Internat.	4/5.7.03	2158
90	Grimshaw, Neville	m	SA	World †	26/27.8.99	2139
91	Tan, Yie Wei	m	Mal	World †	21/22.8.00	2129
92	Zogaj, Idriz	m	S	World	28-30.8.04	2041
93	Cooley, Tatiana	f	USA	World †	21/22.8.00	2023
94	Koblic, Miroslav	m	CZ	National	6.7.02	1990
95	Kopecký, Michal ᴶ	m	CZ	National	6.7.02	1909
96	Kocevar, Christian	m	GER	Internat.	13/14.6.01	1908
97	Amelya, L F. Metta	f	RI	World	3-5.10.03	1892
98	Lancaster, Ralph	m	NZ	National	30.08.03	1888
99	Rosca, Liana ¹·	f	RO	National	28/29.11.03	1879
100	Berger, Denis	m	GER	World †	22-23.08.97	1872

Notes

WMC – Reigning World Memory Champion

J – Junior (13-17 years)

([I]GM) – [International] Grandmaster

(IM) – International Master

1. – Reigning National Memory Champion

K – Kid (up to 12)

Mode of counting

In each of ten disciplines the contestants get points for their performance in relation to the millennium standard in that discipline (= 1000 points); finally all points will be added up.

Types of competition

World Standard Championship
2 – 3 days (10 disciplines with two 1h marathon disciplines)

World Standard Championshipold
2 days (10th discipline = average of nine disciplines)

Internat. Standard Championship
1 – 2 days (30 min marathons instead of 1 h marathons)

Internat. Standard Championshipold
1 – 2 days (10th discipline = average of nine disciplines)

National Standard Championship
1 day (10 disciplines; partly with shorter memo- and recall time)

Regional Standard Championship
1 day (7 disciplines; short disciplines)

Race Memory

In the annals of the history of anthropology, the literature is scattered with references to the 'primitive' method of passing on information from person to person and from generation to generation. The method used throughout the world was primarily storytelling, with no written material to help.

Anthropologists understandably assumed that such a method was far less efficient than the more modern methods of printing, in which the information could be transcribed perfectly, and thus passed on in its original form. Recent observation and research has suggested that perhaps exactly the opposite was true.

Examining the way in which 'modern man' uses literature, it has been observed that a common trend is to wish to rewrite it, in order to stamp the author's own interpretation on the ongoing 'formal memory' of the race. Thus written history has become revised, or completely reinterpreted, and the original fades into the dusty mists of the back shelves of large libraries.

The assumed disintegration of the original spoken tale over generations, on the other hand, is now being seriously questioned. Think, for example, of telling a very small child a fairy tale three or four times. Having done so, tell the child exactly the same story with one word different. What is the reaction of the child?

Invariably an instant 'that's the wrong word' or 'you've used the wrong word!' In other words, the child's memory is perfect, and it will not allow any variation from its original story. This accuracy of narrative memory suggests that the way in which earlier tribes have passed on information may be an almost perfect one, especially if the information is presented in an imaginative and creative way.

Thus you see that, like Homer's epics *The Iliad* and *The Odyssey*, the great memory stories are at the same time great creative inventions.

The more you train your memory, the more you train your creativity. The more you train your creativity, the more you train your memory.

CHAPTER THREE

CHESS

Brief Description

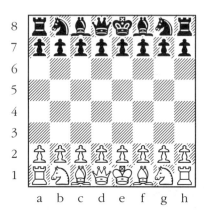

Chess is a board game representing a battle in which the players move alternately, trying to capture (or 'checkmate') the opponent's king.

Chess in its various manifestations can rightly be regarded as the 'king' of board games (along, perhaps, with go). Millions of people around the planet either play chess, are fascinated by it, or follow the exploits of its leading practitioners. The World Chess Federation, FIDE, with 130 member states, is the largest Mind Sports organisation in the world. Chess, shogi and go are capable of making millionaires or even multi-millionaires of their leading exponents. The prize, for example in the 1992 Fischer-Spassky match was a staggering $5 million. And that contest was not even for the official World Championship!

Historical Development

Origins

Chess is said to have originated in India around AD600 under the name 'chaturanga'. This was a word describing the four traditional army units of Indian military forces, namely foot soldiers (pawns), cavalry (knights), chariots (rooks) and elephants (which have come down as bishops in contemporary chess).

The name 'chess' is derived from the Persian word 'Shah', meaning a king or ruler. This word is also related to 'check' and may even be cognate with the words Caesar, Kaiser and Czar, respectively denoting rulers in the Roman Empire, the German Empire and the Russian Empire.

The earliest written reference is from an ancient Persian poem of the late sixth century AD, the *Chatrang Namak*. Chess, in its original (rather slow) form flourished during the Baghdad Caliphate in the tenth century AD. The top player at that time and first chess genius was As-Suli.

The Modern Game

Around 1475 chess underwent a rule change which led to the pieces becoming more dynamic, essentially leading to the Western or 'international' form of the game as we know it. It was at this time that castling was introduced, pawns gained the privilege of advancing two squares on the first move, and the queen was transformed from a waddling cripple of a piece (the Arabic vizier), to one of devastating mobility.

It is doubtless the almost overnight increase in the strength and manoeuvrability of the queen which explains the joyous adventures and excursions with it, the giving of check being particularly popular, whether it advanced a player's cause or not. This can be observed in the recorded games of the new chess up to the early 17th century.

Chess is a game that symbolises warfare, so the increased fire-power of the queen surely reflects the introduction of artillery in the mid-15th century sphere of battlefield technology. The sudden advances in chess must, overall, also be explicable in terms of the Renaissance dynamic, the increasingly urgent perception of distance, space and perspective which distinguishes that phase of human intellectual development. The telescope, the microscope, the use of siege artillery to batter down the walls of Constantinople in 1453, and perspective in art, were all parallel developments.

Columbus discovered the New World for Spain in 1492, and it was fitting that the fresh impetus for chess, as it arose from the tortuous Arabic and medieval form, should also have come from Spain. Why was the spread of the new chess after 1475 so rapid? The answer, often overlooked, is that Spain at that time was the dominant centre for world communication, and thus spread the new chess globally through its explorations and conquests.

The Unofficial World Champions

Before the official title of World Champion was inaugurated in 1886 there were a number of players who could justly claim to be the strongest in the world, although there was not yet a formal championship.

The encounters between the Frenchman La Bourdonnais and McDonnell, who was Irish, were too diffuse to be seen as a real prototype for the modern title matches, although in the year of 1834 the two played no fewer than 88 games. The eventual score was 44 wins to La Bourdonnais and 30 to

McDonnell, with 14 draws. Their play was notable for energy and ferocity rather than finesse.

The first match which closely resembled a modern World Championship was the Staunton-St Amant contest in Paris in 1843, which established an Englishman, Howard Staunton, as the foremost player in the world. Twenty-one games were played and Staunton scored 11 wins to his opponent's six. In 1851 the innovative and indefatigable Staunton organised the first ever international tournament, which was staged in London to coincide with the Great Exhibition held in Hyde Park that year. Participants included Wyvill, Williams and Staunton himself, but the German player Adolf Anderssen was the clear winner.

Seven years later when Paul Morphy, the undisputed American champion, arrived in Europe, he sought matches against the leading continental players and roundly beat Anderssen in a match played in Paris.

In the same year, Staunton met Morphy. It was only a consultation game but there is no doubt, given the crushing nature of Morphy's victory, that the art and science of chess had moved on considerably since Staunton's domination of the game in 1843.

Anderssen had established himself at London in 1851 as, *de facto*, the greatest living master. In 1858, though, Anderssen lost a match to Morphy, but when Morphy retired prematurely Anderssen once again was regarded as the man to beat. The next turning point was the fascinating clash between Anderssen and Steinitz in London in 1866.

The Advent of the 'Official' World Championship Match

During the 1880s Wilhelm Steinitz and Johannes Zukertort had emerged as clearly superior to all of their contemporaries. Both of them claimed to be the strongest player in the world. After a series of bitter verbal exchanges the two men finally met at the chessboard to resolve their conflict. Steinitz scored a decisive victory with ten wins to Zukertort's five.

The outstanding matches in the history of the World Chess Championship have, by general consent, been those which exhibited a fierce contrast in the playing style of the two protagonists. At the very dawn of recognised World Championship play in 1886 the fiery imagination and tactical arsenal of Johannes Zukertort, although meeting with initial resounding successes, ultimately foundered on the rock hard strategic logic of the new scientific school propounded by Wilhelm Steinitz. After a series of fascinating games Steinitz was declared the first official chess champion of the world.

The new champion held the title until 1894, when he lost a match to the rising German star Emanuel Lasker. A second defeat at Lasker's hands in 1896 was, perhaps, a partial cause of Steinitz's suffering a nervous breakdown, from which he never fully recovered. He died in a state of poverty as a public ward of the City of New York in 1900.

Steinitz was the chief promoter of the 'modern' school of chess, a system which rejected the pyrotechnics of sacrifices and combinations, concentrating instead on positional play aimed at the accumulation of small advantages. Yet Steinitz, too, was to meet his master eventually in the shape of Emanuel Lasker. For all his strategic skill Steinitz could not cope with the slippery shifting pragmatism of Lasker's style, a style possessed of such flexibility and resilience that it was to maintain Lasker's grip on the supreme title until 1921, when he was defeated by the Cuban genius Capablanca. However, when Lasker and Capablanca had first clashed at St Petersburg in 1914, Lasker proved the stronger.

Kasparov's Chess Idol

Garry Kasparov, who is generally regarded as the greatest player ever, has often stated that Alexander Alekhine is his chess hero. Their stylistic resemblance is clear to see. Both love combinations and the attack, though in 1927, when Alekhine had to face the virtually invincible Capablanca for the World Championship, he curbed his natural predilections in order to become a super-strategist. Kasparov had to learn the same lesson when struggling against Karpov six decades later.

From 1927 until 1946 (with a two-year gap after his defeat in the first match against the Dutch Grandmaster Max Euwe) the genius Alexander Alekhine held sway over the chess world. Alekhine had a style so multi-faceted that he could overmatch Capablanca in the Cuban champion's own blend of trench warfare and victory by attrition. Nevertheless, Alekhine was far more at home in the confused tactical melees which characterised his four matches from 1929 until 1937 against Bogoljubow and Euwe.

During the 1950's chess was dominated by the Soviet School, exemplified by Botvinnik and Smyslov, players so close in style that their games were hardly distinguishable from each other. It was not until 1960, when the vibrant young Latvian Mikhail Tal inflicted a crushing defeat on Mikhail Botvinnik, that the stylistic clash to be found at the core of great matches once again became truly visible. Botvinnik's Olympian calm was repeatedly shattered by the Napoleonic force of the young Tal: their games were replete with grand strategic designs occasionally triumphing, but more often collapsing under the variegated assault of tempestuous tactical sorties. For connoisseurs, the two matches between Botvinnik and Tal in 1960 and 1961 represented some of the most bloodthirsty and exciting chess seen at World Championship level. Although he was defeated in the first match Botvinnik, employing subtle psychology, triumphed in the second, exploiting Tal's dislike of simplification and the endgame.

Mikhail Botvinnik had won the World Championship in 1948, finishing ahead of Smyslov, Reshevsky, Keres and Euwe in the quintangular match tournament held to determine the new champion after Alekhine had died in possession of the title.

The Soviet School

During the 1950s and early 1960s Botvinnik had to fight off challenges from Mikhail Tal, as well as David Bronstein, Vassily Smyslov and Tigran Petrosian.

Smyslov drew with Botvinnik in 1954, seized the championship in 1957 but a year later succumbed in Botvinnik's revenge match. As we have seen, Tal also briefly deposed Botvinnik, only to lose the title back in a revenge match. It was Petrosian, in 1963, who eventually and definitively unseated Botvinnik from the world throne, and this time Botvinnik did not have the right to a revenge match!

A Western World Champion

Although Petrosian narrowly succeeded in defending the title in against Boris Spassky in 1966, he eventually relinquished it to Spassky in 1969. Spassky in turn was usurped by the unpredictable American Bobby Fischer in a titanic match in Reykjavik in 1972. Spassky was an adventurous attacker. His play was very much in the mould of Tal and Alekhine, yet in Fischer he succumbed to the prophet of heroic materialism. Fischer was a chess superman who would snatch material in a fashion that might have seemed sordid in a lesser player, only to release it at the appropriate moment for overwhelming advantages in terms of the initiative, mobility and striking power. It was a tragedy for the world of chess that Fischer ceded the title by default to Anatoly Karpov in 1975 and did not play a single serious tournament or match game for the two decades from 1972 to 1992.

Paul Morphy

Paul Morphy was born in New Orleans in 1837 and developed an exceptional talent from an early age – at 13 he was already established as one of America's leading players. He came to Europe in 1858 and, to everybody's surprise, defeated the cream of European chess: Lowenthal, Harrwitz and Anderssen were all overwhelmed in matches over a six-month period.

Morphy was able to reach these astronomical heights in chess with relatively little traditional-style study of the game, because he was able to depend upon a naturally studied and developed ability to make images and to translate this into an astonishingly powerful memory. Like Bidder, Heinecken, Magliabechi, and others before him, Morphy used the base of his knowledge to extend himself into other fields, acquiring on his way to the chess championship, four different languages and a degree in law.

Morphy also distinguished himself in another extraordinary mental memory field: blindfold chess. Morphy developed this skill to play many simultaneous games blindfolded – a mental test which requires a perfect recall of every new position in every simultaneous game. He also applied his memory to law and could recite verbatim most of the Civil Law Code of Louisiana.

As his fame spread, so did knowledge of his claim that he could remember the moves of every championship game he had ever played in his life. People scoffed at this claim, but it was not put to the test. Then one day it was realised that records of over 400 of his games had been lost, so Morphy simply sat down and wrote out the lot! His opponents and referees of the games subsequently confirmed that all the reconstructions he had made were exact.

The remarkable skill that Morphy exhibited is an example of a talent that can be developed in every memory – the ability to retrieve in detail the most complex of memory events, even those which may appear to have been lost forever, but which the remarkable brain retains perfectly.

The Greatest Rivalry

After successfully defending the title twice against the Soviet defector Viktor Korchnoi, Karpov had to face a fresh challenge in 1984 from Garry Kasparov, whose rise to challenger status had been nothing less than meteoric. Their first match ended in controversial circumstances, when the FIDE (World Chess Federation) President, Florencio Campomanes, stopped the match after more than five month's play, claiming exhaustion on the part of contestants and organisers. Kasparov disputed this decision vehemently and accused Campomanes of coming to Karpov's aid just when Kasparov was looking as if he might snatch victory from the jaws of defeat. This injustice must have spurred Kasparov to greater efforts, for in the return match in 1985 he seized the title in dramatic fashion to become the youngest World Champion in history. Since 1985 Kasparov successfully defended against Karpov on three occasions, the final one being the 1990 match, split between New York and Lyons. The apparent narrowness of Kasparov's margin of victory is illusory. Kasparov had the match wrapped up by game 22, but slipped back to lose game 23 after he had already decided the contest in his favour. After this match Karpov was defeated by Nigel Short in the elimination cycle and the challenger baton was passed to the young Englishman. Short lost to Kasparov in 1993, and Kasparov defended his title again in 1995 against Anand of India. In London 2000, Kasparov lost the World Championship title to Vladimir Kramnik, but has retained his ranking (even in his current retirement) as the world number one.

Garry Kasparov – The Greatest Player Ever

Just how great is Garry Kasparov? His commitment to not only remain so but increasingly to accelerate away from his rivals, appears nearly absolute. Despite his distaste for losing, he is courageous enough to take risks, to explore new creative variations and to learn from his mistakes. Renowned for his mental literacy, including a phenomenal memory, a laser-like analysis, and an extraordinary imagination, he describes his approach to the game: 'From the very beginning of a game, I strive to make it as sharp as possible and to take it outside the familiar patterns.'

Kasparov's knowledge of the game is becoming legendary, and his mastermind group includes not only many of the world's best chess coaches, but now a vast computer databank of tens of thousands of games and positional analyses.

His attitude towards himself and his abilities in the game exudes self-confidence, and is the one area in which his opponents see possible signs of a weakness – that he may fall into the psychological trap of thinking he is invincible and thus will neither prepare nor stay in physical and mental shape. Time will tell.

Kasparov's love of the game extends well beyond the competitive chess-board. Believing, with Goethe, that chess is 'the touchstone of the intellect', Kasparov has supported initiatives in schools, including The Brain Trust's Chess League for Schools, in the belief that the playing of chess by children develops all their cortical skills, as well as encouraging social interaction, promulgating teamwork and co-operation, and teaching them the value both of friendly competition and learning from both mistakes and successes.

Kasparov's energy and persistence are similarly extraordinary. Meeting him is often described as 'like having your hand put into a socket and having all your lights turned on!' His persistence was demonstrated in his first World Championship match against Karpov, where he came back from five games down and over a period of three solid months of the highest level of combat (indeed he describes chess as 'an art, a science and a sport') he ground down the world's second-ranked player of all-time to such an extent that both mentally and physically Karpov was incapable of continuing.

To succeed continually at this level, Kasparov has to be superbly fit physically. Only aerobic fitness can provide what is needed when considering the hundreds of variations on the 52nd move of the 23rd game in a two-month long conflict that will decide the future of the thinker's life. He is the supreme example amongst Mind Sports practitioners of *mens sana in corpore sano* (healthy body, healthy mind).

Chess Records

Top Ten World Chess Federation (FIDE) Ratings of All-Time

Rank	Player (country)	Rating	Dates
1	Garry Kasparov (Russia)	2815	1963-
2	Bobby Fischer (USA)	2785	1943-
3=	Anatoly Karpov (Russia)	2775	1951-
3=	Vladimir Kramnik (Russia)	2775	1975-
5	Viswanathan Anand(India)	2765	1969-
6	Veselin Topalov (Bulgaria)	2750	1975-
7	Gata Kamsky (USA)	2745	1974-
8	Vassily Ivanchuk (Ukraine)	2740	1969-
9	José Raoul Capablanca (Cuba)	2725	1888-1942
10=	Mikhail Botvinnik (USSR)	2720	1911-1995
10=	Emanuel Lasker (Germany)	2720	1868-1941

Professor Nathan Divinsky ranks the following top ten, according solely to their games over an extended period and only against the elite.

Rank	Player (country)
1	Garry Kasparov (Russia)
2	Anatoly Karpov (Russia)
3	Bobby Fischer (USA)
4	Mikhail Botvinnik (USSR)
5	José Raoul Capablanca (Cuba)
6	Emanuel Lasker (Germany)
7	Viktor Korchnoi (USSR and Switzerland)
8	Boris Spassky (USSR and France)
9	Vassily Smyslov (Russia)
10	Tigran Petrosian (Armenia)

World Champions

Year	Champion (country)
1886-1894	Wilhelm Steinitz (Austria)
1894-1921	Emanuel Lasker (Germany)
1921-1927	José Raoul Capablanca (Cuba)
1927-1935	Alexander Alekhine (Russia/France)
1935-1937	Max Euwe (Holland)
1937-1946	Alexander Alekhine (Russia/France)
1948-1957	Mikhail Botvinnik (USSR)
1957-1958	Vassily Smyslov (USSR)
1958-1960	Mikhail Botvinnik (USSR)
1960-1961	Mikhail Tal (USSR)
1961-1963	Mikhail Botvinnik (USSR)
1963-1969	Tigran Petrosian (USSR)
1969-1972	Boris Spassky (USSR/France)
1972-1975	Robert Fischer (USA)
1975-1985	Anatoly Karpov (USSR/Russia)
1985-2000	Garry Kasparov (USSR/Russia)
2000-	Vladimir Kramnik (USSR/Russia)

Top Ten Current Players (May 2005)

Rank	Player (country)	Elo rating
1	Garry Kasparov (Russia)	2812
2	Viswanathan Anand (India)	2785
3	Veselin Topalov (Bulgaria)	2778
4	Peter Leko (Hungary)	2753
5	Vladimir Kramnik (Russia)	2740
6	Vassily Ivanchuk (Ukraine)	2739
7	Michael Adams (England)	2737
8	Judith Polgar (Hungary)	2732
9	Etienne Bacrot (France)	2731
10	Peter Svidler (Russia)	2725

The Times Poll

The above lists define the greatest chess players purely on the basis of results. Individual results are, of course, important, but one also has to consider other factors such as: the ability to rise to the supremely significant occasion, persistence in playing record, the ability to inspire and teach, and also sheer brilliance of play. If one takes such considerations into account the results will be different.

My own (Raymond Keene) personal list for the 12 greatest players of all time would read as follows: Kasparov, Lasker, Botvinnik, Capablanca, Alekhine, Fischer, Morphy, Steinitz, Petrosian, Karpov, Tal and Anderssen. In 2004, I conducted a poll, through the chess column in *The Times* (London) newspaper, asking readers to name their own personal Top 12 list. The results were combined with the 'number one' nominations receiving 12 points, the 'number two' 11 points etc, down to 1 point for being 'number 12'. When all the scores were added up, the following list resulted.

Rank	Player (country)	Points
1	Garry Kasparov (Russia)	590
2	Bobby Fischer (USA)	521
3	Jose Capablanca (Cuba)	477
4	Alexander Alekhine (Russia/France)	444
5	Emanuel Lasker (Germany)	411
6	Mikhail Botvinnik (USSR)	302
7	Anatoly Karpov (USSR/Russia)	255
8	Mikhail Tal (USSR)	219
9	Paul Morphy (USA)	199
10	Wilhelm Steinitz (Austria)	163
11	Tigran Petrosian (USSR)	152
12	Vassily Smyslov (USSR)	77

Longest Reign as World Champion

Dr Emanuel Lasker, from 1894 to 1921 – 26 years, 337 days.

Youngest World Champion

On 9 November 1985 Garry Kasparov (b. 13 April 1963) defeated Anatoly Karpov in Moscow. Kasparov's precise age: 22 years, 210 days.

Strongest Woman Player

Hungarian Judit Polgar is the strongest woman player ever by some margin. She currently (July 2005) has a rating of 2735, placing her 8th in the world.

Youngest Women's World Champion

The Georgian Maya Chiburdanidze became Women's World Champion in 1978 at the age of 17, a title she held until 1991.

Youngest Grandmaster

On 20 August 2002, the Ukranian Sergei Karjakin shocked the chess world by fulfilling his third and final GM norm at the international tournament in Sudak. This made him the youngest grandmaster in chess history, at the age of 12 years and 7 months.

Youngest Victories against a Titled Player

(World and US Record) Samuel Reshevsky, aged 10, beat Grandmaster David Janowsky in the New York tournament of 1922; Nine-year-old Gawain Jones defeated International Master Malcolm Pein at the Stockton tournament in 1997.

Oldest World Champion

Wilhelm Steinitz (b. 1836) who won the title in 1886 and held on to it until losing to Lasker on 26 May 1894. Champion at 58 years and 10 days.

Mind Sports as Sports...

The most common argument for not counting chess as a sport is that it does not demand physical exercise. However that statement should be questioned.

The authors recall a small experiment in the 1960's. Over a competition weekend (two and a half days) some players tried to eat, exercise and sleep just as much as they had the previous weekend. The previous weekend they had, however, read, watched TV, etc., instead of participating in a chess competition.

One of the players, by playing 6-9 hours of chess per day, lost almost 2.5 kg (or over 5 lb) of his body weight during the competition weekend. And it was documented that during the 1984/85 match against Garry Kasparov, which lasted five months, Anatoly Karpov lost 9 kg (20 lb)!

In fact, intense mental exercise can be quite demanding physically – at least in terms of burning calories.

Most Invincible Player

José Raoul Capablanca lost just 34 games out of 571 during his career as a chessplayer from 1909 to 1939. He established the amazing feat of remaining unbeaten over 63 master and grandmaster level games, including a World Championship match – from 10 February 1916 to 21 March 1924.

In modern times, Vladimir Kramnik went unbeaten over 83 games, played in a period of 18 months leading up to July 2000. These games were played in a variety of tournaments, but the majority were against world class opposition.

Simultaneous Marathon World Record

On 5-6 October 1984, the Czech Grandmaster Vlastimil Hort played against 663 opponents, on a replacement basis, over a period of 32½ hours at Porz, Germany.

On 6 January 1996, in Alvsjo, Sweden, Grandmaster Ulf Andersson played against 311 opponents simultaneously. He took 15 hours and 23 minutes to win 269, draw 40, and lose just two.

The record is currently held by English international master Andrew Martin. On 21 February 2004, at Wellington College Crowthorne, he played 321 chess players all at the same time. His score on the day was: 294 wins, 26 draws and just one loss. Andrew started the record attempt at 09.27 and did not finish until 02.18 next day. During this 16 hour 51 minute marathon, he walked over 5 miles and played over 7,000 moves in total. Andrew recorded his first win at 10.45, reached his 80% target wins at 00.55.

Consecutive Marathon World Record

Master player Graham Burgess took 72 hours from Wednesday 18 May until Saturday 21 May 1994, at the London Chess Centre, Euston, to win 431 games, draw 25 and lose 54, for an 87% score against opposition rated 1855 on average.

Blindfold World Record

On 1 February 1925 in Paris, Alexander Alekhine played 28 boards simultaneously blindfold, scoring 22 wins, three losses and three draws. Although later players have slightly surpassed Alekhine's total of opponents, Alekhine's display against players of national master strength is regarded as having provided the greatest standard of opposition for such an exhibition.

Harry Nelson Pillsbury, the American Grandmaster (1872-1906) regularly played 12 games of chess and six games of draughts at the same time, without sight of the boards, whilst simultaneously playing one hand of (sighted) whist. Before one such display he also memorised 30 strange words, which he was able to recall perfectly forwards and backwards at the end.

The World Champions – a New Roll of Honour

Introduction

Garry Kasparov's publishing phenomenon *My Great Predecessors* is revolution-ising the way we think about world champions. According to the authority of Kasparov himself, he was the 13th champion in direct succession from the first incumbent, Steinitz. His title was passed on, again in direct linear suc-cession, to the 14th, Kramnik, who defeated Kasparov hinmself in London 2000 and who in 2004 defended the championship in Switzerland against the Hungarian Grandmaster and challenger, Peter Leko.

What Kasparov's series has openly admitted, though, is what fair-minded observers have known for some time, namely that there are a number of Steinitz's precursors who pioneered the world championship match format and were legitimately recognised as the world's best in their own day. The complicating factor for the formulation of the official title was, to a certain extent, an *interregnum* after the death of Labourdonnais in 1840. An even greater obstacle, however, resided in Paul Morphy's domination of his con-temporaries in the late 1850s, vitiated by his refusal to play a single important match until his death a quarter of a century later.

Steinitz has the longest reign!

Steinitz, who was according to tradition, 'officially' crowned the first world champion after his match victory against Zukertort in 1886, claimed himself that his reign had actually commenced in 1866 – with Morphy alive but inac-tive – when he overcame Adolph Anderssen in a set match in London. If we date Steinitz's tenure from then, his record as champion also opens up to embrace match wins against Blackburne and a crushing previous encounter against Zukertort in 1872, thus granting us a much more rounded view of Steinitz's achievements. This also has the effect of making Steinitz the record holder as world champion with 27 years as opposed to Lasker's 26! And if we include these results we should, of course, also consider the claims of those other dominating colossi of their day, Morphy, Anderssen himself, Staunton and Labourdonnais as serious contenders in the pantheon of champions. Labourdonnais in 1834 paved the way for the modern world championship match as we know it. Before then, only Philidor comes into consideration, but there are greater difficulties in declaring him the strongest player of his day.

At this time of turmoil in world chess, the chess community has a superb opportunity to recognise the Labourdonnais-McDonnell matches as the first world title contest. They stand out so clearly in extent, importance and quality from anything that ever went before them that they are the overwhelmingly most attractive moment from which to derive the remainder of our world championship history. From that clash, there is a clear line of succession:

Labourdonnais vs McDonnell 1834

Staunton vs. St. Amant 1843.

Staunton vs. Harrwitz 1846.

Staunton vs. Horwitz 1846.

Staunton vs. Anderssen 1851 (plus the vitally important fact that Anderssen went on to win the 1851 tournament).

Anderssen vs. Morphy 1858.

Steinitz vs. Anderssen 1866.

…and then Steinitz all the way until the familiar succession of Lasker.

The corrected dispensation in the line of champions would, therefore, now look like this:

Years	Champion
1834-1840	Labourdonnais (died after 6 years as champion)
1840-1843	Interregnum, though French school still regarded as dominant
1843-1851	Staunton accedes to title, beating leading Frenchman St. Amant
1851-1858	Anderssen wins London 1851 beating Staunton in the process
1858-1860	Morphy (withdrew from active chess after 1859)
1860-1866	Interregnum, though Morphy still regarded as champion
1866-1894	Steinitz defeats Anderssen after seven years of Morphy dormancy
1894-1921	Lasker
1921-1927	Capablanca
1927-1935	Alekhine
1935-1937	Euwe

Years	Champion
1927-1935	Alekhine who dies in possession of title
1946-1948	Interregnum, World Federation backed by USSR appropriates title
1948-1957	Botvinnik
1957-1958	Smyslov
1958-1960	Botvinnik
1960-1961	Tal
1961-1963	Botvinnik
1963-1969	Petrosian
1969-1972	Spassky
1972-1975	Fischer
1975-1985	Karpov
1985-2000	Kasparov – last three title defences outside FIDE jurisdiction
2000-??	Kramnik

The two big changes stemming from this revision are:.

1) We end up with 18 champions, not 14 – adding Labourdonnais, Staunton, Morphy and Anderssen. This constitutes an outstanding group to join the champions'club.

2) Steinitz becomes the longest holder of the title, replacing Lasker. His record of match wins before he lost to Lasker – against Anderssen, Blackburne, Zukertort (twice), Tchigorin (twice) and Gunsberg now looks enormously impressive.

Evidence for – and problems with – this view are discussed below.

Discontinuities

What about unnatural breaks and schism? Admittedly, these bedevil our revised early history of the championship, but they have also disrupted the modern game.

Labourdonnais died a natural death without facing Staunton. After the demise of Labourdonnais, the *Tricolore* was upheld against the British challenge by the leading representative of the French School, St. Amant.

Morphy declined to play Steinitz, who dated his accession to the title to his defeat of Anderssen in 1866.

Botvinnik was deprived of a match against Alekhine by the latter's premature death; FIDE asserts its authority over the vacant title.

Fischer, emulating Morphy, refused to accept a challenge, on this occasion from Karpov, who was declared champion by FIDE.

Every other handover from one champion to the next has been marked by a direct contest between the two.

It is not possible, even if it were desirable, to resolve the status of the championship during the periods of *interregnum*; however, it does not invalidate the idea of there being a position of world champion which we can trace back through these periods to more definite situations.

Starting Date – Problems with Philidor

Before the Labourdonnais-McDonnell match of 1834 there are really no games or records of matches that can support the idea of a dominating champion. Everyone in England and France looked up to Philidor, but he had strong Italian contemporaries and critics such as Ercole del Rio, Ponziani , Lolli and Cozio whom he never met and who happened to disagree violently with his theories. We have no record at all of any serious world championship-style match until De Labourdonnais plays McDonnell. Then the die is cast and the future template for matches set. Staunton's three matches (against St. Amant, Horwitz and Harrwitz) are in fact remarkably similar in form to modern world championship matches.

So, our revision embraces Labourdonnais as the first recognised champion, then Staunton, Anderssen Morphy and Steinitz (but from 1866 not 1886).

'Champions' before 1886

Each of the 'new' additions to the start of the list was regarded as 'champion' in their day, and oftentimes since.

In 1834, when Labourdonnais played McDonnell, the assiduous scribe George Walker made it obvious in his writings and his collection of the games that these were the finest ever played and that Labourdonnais was the supreme chessplayer wherever the game was played. I think the criterion must be – what did the chessplayers and the public think at the time? Our view is that they were all very well aware of the notion of a supreme champion but they further regarded this concept as being the champion of all chessplayers wherever they were.

The series between Labourdonnais and McDonnell in London 1834 was hailed by experts at the time as the best ever and the winner as superior, even, to the legendary Philidor. Labourdonnais' reputation was, if anything, enhanced by a narrow 13-12 match loss against the powerful Hungarian master Szen at Paris in 1836. The enhancement was because Labourdonnais was offering the scarcely believable odds of pawn and two moves to his illustrious opponent!

In 1951, Wade and Winter, in their book on Botvinnik vs. Bronstein, claim Staunton vs. St. Amant 1843 to have been the first official world championship match. So there is good authority for considering this match as part of the chain of succession, although we need not accede to their view that it was the first in line.

It has been widely accepted that it was Steinitz who invented the phrase *world chess champion* , but the notion itself certainly predated him by at least 32 years. For example, in 1844 in Bristol and again at the Yorkshire chess association dinner of 1845, Staunton was hailed officially and in public as 'the champion.' From the context, it was obvious that they meant champion of all chessplayers, not just British ones.

We should further add that the respected Dutch chess historian Dr P. Feenstra Kuiper pronounced that the 1858 Morphy vs. Anderssen match was certainly for world supremacy: *'Man kann ruhig sagen, dass dieser Wettkampf...um die Weltmeisterschaft gekaempft wurde.'*. One can say without fear of contradiction that this was a genuine world championship contest.

Steinitz personally claimed 1866 for the start of his tenure of the title. The contract between the players for the 1886 match refers to it being for the chess championship of the world – but nowhere is it claimed that this is the first such match!

Before 1886, Steinitz defeated Anderssen in a match in 1866, then crushed Zukertort and annihilated Blackburne 7-0. By defeating these three, he did as much as he could to meet the strongest players of the day in matches. It would be interesting to track down exactly where Steinitz made the 1866 claim! In *The Field* of July 18, 1874, Steinitz refers to himself as 'the champion' – exactly the same phrase used to describe Staunton.

It is clear that Steinitz regarded Anderssen as having been the champion, that the title became Morphy's property when he beat Anderssen but that because of Morphy's inactivity it had reverted back to being Anderssen's again.

However, Steinitz should not be taken as the sole authority on this matter – what did the rest of the chess world think? We might reasonably take J.J. Lowenthal to be the voice of the chess establishment until he died in 1874. He recognised Steinitz publicly as 'the occupant of the exceptional position formerly held by Morphy '(1873).

Similarly, Amos Burn, a grandmaster-strength player, also announced that Steinitz was the 'strongest living player' around the same time – that is, well before 1886.

Even in 1896, top experts such as Pollock and Mason were quite clear in their book on the St. Petersburg tournament that the title at least went back to Steinitz-Anderssen 1866. Their view is that the line stretches back even earlier – they quote Labourdonnais, Staunton, Anderssen and Morphy as champions. This shows that even quite near the time, the 1886 date had no special significance amongst the leading players and writers.

Dr Milan Vidmar, in his memoirs *Goldene Schachzeiten*, is also very clear on this point. He asserts that:.

'Steinitz held the world championship for a record 28 years – while Lasker was number 2 with 27' (actually it should be 27 plus and 26 plus respectively but the point he is making is trenchant enough).

The collective evidence that the chess fraternity knew who was 'the champion' at any given moment is overwhelming.

This strange divide we have built up around 1886 mainly serves to do a terrible injustice to Steinitz – his reign was longer than Lasker's and he did contest nine matches for the title against the best possible opposition over 28 years – an average of one match every three years! In fact –something you cannot even say of Lasker, who missed Rubinstein and Pillsbury – Steinitz faced every conceivable opponent of title calibre over his 28 years – three of them twice! He even challenged Tarrasch... who turned Steinitz down.

Morphy as Champion

It seems increasingly ridiculous to exclude Morphy from the champions when he was far and away the most crushing force the chess world had ever seen before. We have cited above one contemporary view that regarded his match with Anderssen as being for recognition as the best player in the world.

Recently, we predicted that if we looked at the speeches made/articles published in the USA on Morphy's return from his triumphant tour of Europe in 1858 they would make it abundantly clear that he was regarded as the champion! Sure enough, researcher Louis Blair was assiduous enough to discover:.

'According to Lawson's Morphy biography, it was reported in the June 1, 1859 *Boston Journal* that Dr. Oliver Wendell Holmes referred to Morphy as 'the world's Chess Champion'. Lawson also mentioned a May 26, 1859 *New York Times* report that John Van Buren declared that Morphy was 'the Chess

Champion of the World'. (www.chesschamps.com)

So much for the myth that Steinitz invented the title! It was then thought that Morphy's continual presence , even though inactive, would have annihilated any claims Steinitz made on the championship before 1886. But , on the contrary, Morphy was regarded as retired and Steinitz was seen as the champion. Again we refer to assiduous researcher Louis Blair , who has disinterred the following remark:

'as Mr. Morphy no longer considers himself a chessplayer, there is no reason why others should do so.' – *The Chess World* (edited by Staunton) 1866.

We also see little evidence in the 19th century of the kind of fanaticism which a century later insisted on calling Fischer world champion well past his sell-by date. When Morphy stopped playing serious chess after defeating Anderssen, the top players suffered few illusions that he would return. By contrast, Anderssen's continued top-level activity, beating Kolisch in a match and winning London 1862, swiftly re-established him as the top man.

Even if we accept that Morphy's shadow might have prevented Steinitz from declaring himself world champion before 1886, that has no effect all on the prior standing as champions of Labourdonnais, Staunton, Anderssen and Morphy himself. The question of whether we accept these four as champions is different – though connected – from whether the reign of Steinitz began in 1866 or 1886!

Ranking the Champions

Discussions of who was the greatest ever player are perennially intellectually stimulating but naturally will often collapse into partisan declarations of faith or endless gnawing at historical bones of diverse provenance. However, we can bring a little science to this debate, and the results of one particular approach are presented below.

We have conducted the exercise of taking all the official champions, plus those both we and Kasparov recognise as legitimate precursors, and analysed their results amongst themselves. We now have a pool of eighteen names. We arranged them in order, awarding 36 points for number one, down to two for number eighteen, based on the percentages scored in all contests which might be considered to have been for the title. Thus we included Staunton's thunderous series of 1840s match wins against the European masters St. Amant, Horwitz and Harrwitz, but excluded a Steinitz match win vs. Blackburne which predated 1866, Steinitz's own date for his accession to the Purple. For Morphy, we have included solely his final match victory – against Anderssen – which confirmed the American genius as the world's best player at that time (1858).

From this calculation of percentages scored, Morphy emerged on top with 36 points, while Euwe came in last with 2. We further awarded a score from 1-18, based on strength of opposition within the group, based on the afore-mentioned percentages. At this stage, Capablanca added a bonus of 18, while Morphy with 2 and Labourdonnais 1 brought up the rear. Finally, we re-peated this exercise to award a further set of points (1-18) predicated on the number of games played, thus assessing relative persistence within the group. In this case, Kasparov notched an extra 18 points, while Morphy added just 1 to his tally.

Rank	Player	Points
1	Lasker	58
2	Steinitz	53
3	Kasparov	46
4	Alekhine	46
5	Labourdonnais	44
6	Karpov	40
7	Staunton	40
8	Botvinnik	39
9	Morphy	39
10	Kramnik	38
11	Smyslov	37
12	Fischer	37
13	Capablanca	36
14	Petrosian	29
15	Euwe	27
16	Spassky	27
17	Anderssen	25
18	Tal	23

The final scores are illuminating. While we would by no means claim that Labourdonnais or Staunton were truly stronger than Tal, the scores certainly do suggest that we should pay more attention to such giants of the past, and in particular to Steinitz, whose record before 1886 tends to be overlooked in the shadow of the inactive Morphy, much as Karpov was later undervalued while Fischer remained dormant but potentially active. Ties in the list have been broken by virtue of the stronger opposition within the group. Lasker comes out on top because, compared to the others, he scored an overall high percentage including all his championship matches, earning 34 points, faced powerful opposition, confined to rivals strictly within the group (a further 11 points) and played a large number of overall games for the title, thus earning himself a further 13 point bonus.

What makes this chart of particular interest is that it only includes games that truly mattered; no exhibition, training or isolated tournament games dilute their potency. Each and every game evaluated here was to establish the protagonists' position in the world hierarchy and place in chess history.

Man v Machine

Chessplaying computer programs have been able to compete with the world's best human players since 1996. The first such match was a six-game encounter between IBM's Deep Blue and Garry Kasparov in Philadelphia 1996. Deep Blue sensationally won the first game but Kasparov fought back and took the match comfortably by the score of 4-2.

In 1997 a rematch was played in New York. Deep Blue was now able to assess 200,000,000 positions per second and IBM had hired a team of four grandmasters to help with preparation. Nevertheless, following on from his previous victory, Kasparov was the hot favourite to win. He got off to a good start, winning the first game, but Deep Blue squared the match with a win in the next game. The machine went on to win sensationally by the score of 3½-2½ when Kasparov crashed to a horrible 19 move defeat in the final game. The event was a phenomenal media success and received blanket coverage throughout the world. IBM even received the supreme accolade of being publicly congratulated by Microsoft. IBM declined offers of a rematch and immediately terminated the 'Deep Blue project'.

The next two matches were held in 2002 and saw two commercial chess software packages (albeit running on very powerful hardware) take on the world numbers one and two: Garry Kasparov and Vladimir Kramnik. The first match was between Kramnik and Deep Fritz and was held at the Mind Sports and Dama Centre in Bahrain. This eight game match ended in a 4-4 tie. Later in the year, Kasparov took on Deep Junior in a six game match in New York and this clash was also drawn, 3-3.

In 2003 Kasparov and Deep fritz played out a 2-2 tie in a mini-match in New York.

In 2004 the sensational Kasparov-Deep Blue match was revisited with the worldwide release of the film, Game Over: Kasparov versus Deep Blue, by Indian director Vikram Jayanti.

2005 saw the arrival of a new chesplaying machine, Hydra. Hydra was paired against the British number one Michael Adams in a six-game match in London. The result was a crushing 5½-½ win for the machine against a player consistently ranked in the world's top six for many years.

CHAPTER FOUR

SHOGI (JAPANESE CHESS)

Brief Description

	9	8	7	6	5	4	3	2	1	
一	香	桂	銀	金	王	金	銀	桂	香	一
		飛						角		二
三	歩	歩	歩	歩	歩	歩	歩	歩	歩	三
										四
										五
										六
七	歩	歩	歩	歩	歩	歩	歩	歩	歩	七
		角						飛		八
九	香	桂	銀	金	玉	金	銀	桂	香	九

In the past few years, sumo wrestling has become widely popular as a spectator sport in the west. Now Japan is exporting a more esoteric, indigenous pastime as increasing numbers of occidentals are taking up shogi, the distinctive home-grown Japanese national board game and their version of chess. In Japan there are a staggering 15 million regular shogi players, every newspaper has a daily column and television offers a weekly instructional programme of ninety minutes duration. Sponsorship, which comes mainly from newspaper syndicates, is big business, with top professionals earning something approaching £1 million in one season. Earnings derive from prize money, salaries, game fees and royalties from books. Top shogi players are sufficiently well known to feature regularly in TV advertising, promoting a range of products. In Japan the public image of shogi combines the popularity and glamour of snooker with the intellectual rigours of chess.

Shogi is played on a 9x9 board with 20 flat, wedge-shaped pieces per side. It has many elements that will be readily recognisable to the chessplayer. In both games the aim is to checkmate the opposing king. Shogi players each have a king, a rook, a bishop and nine pawns, all of which move in the same way as their chess counterparts, but the knights are more restricted in scope. Shogi also sports the romantically named golds, silvers and lances, whose moves have no chess equivalent.

Most shogi pieces have the power of promotion, which in chess is confined to pawns alone, but undoubtedly the most striking feature of the Japanese game is the 'drop' which allows a piece captured from an opponent to be dropped back onto the board at strategic moments to reinforce attacks and defences. Captured pieces in shogi never vanish permanently from the board but instead defect to the enemy. This perhaps indicates that when shogi was being developed it accurately reflected the behaviour of real-life Japanese mercenary armies on the battlefield.

The diagram on the previous page depicts the original Japanese pieces while the following diagram shows their modern Western equivalents.

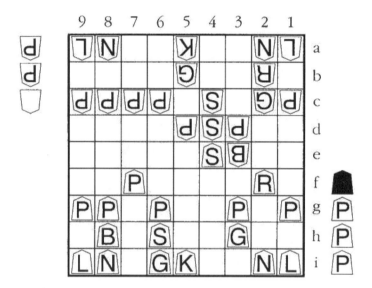

Historical Development

Origins

Shogi does have common roots with the western game of chess as we know it today. A branch of chess reached Japan in the eighth century AD and underwent 'improvements', much as chess did in the west. In the mid-fourteenth century stronger pieces were introduced to the shogi board and promotions and 'drops' were added. The earliest game score extant under the present rules was played in 1607 – and in 1612 a Board of Shogi was set up and the leading players were awarded handsome annual salaries from the government. These players formed an hereditary caste in society. They and their descendants (by birth or adoption) studied shogi as a full-time pursuit and entertained the Shogun annually on the 17th November in the ceremonial castle games played in the Edo Palace. The leading player of the day was recognised by the title Meijin, which was a lifetime appointment. This system continued until 1862.

The Modern Game

At the end of the last century newspaper proprietors took over as the patrons of the top shogi players and there followed a period of factionalism concerning entitlement to the Meijin title, which was only settled after the foundation of the Japanese Shogi Federation in the 1920s. In 1937 the title of Meijin became the property of the Federation, who arranged for annual title matches, thus ushering in the modern tournament scene. It is fascinating to observe that much the same thing – transfer of ownership of title from an individual to a Federation, occurred in shogi, chess and go, in the same decade 1937-1946!

The newspapers retain a firm foothold in the shogi world by sponsoring professional tournaments. This gives them the exclusive rights to publish the game scores from these events.

The Professional Scene

Currently there are about 150 professional shogi players in Japan, who compete for the Meijin title in league matches, with promotion and relegation. A new player enters the lowest league and must work his way up, taking at least five years to qualify for the Meijin match. The most recent match saw 33-year-old Habu Yoshiharu, the dominant player of the 1990s, lose the title to 33-year-old Moriuchi Toshiyuki, a rival since childhood. In recent months Moriuchi has won 3 title matches against Habu to become the leading figure in the shogi world.

At the level of top title matches each player is allotted an astounding nine hours thinking time. When this allocation is used up he is given a certain amount of time per move, usually a minute, and this is known as *byoyomi*, literally 'second-counting', as the timekeeper counts out the time aloud. The time taken to complete a top-class game contributes to the general aura of intellectual concentration that is associated with shogi. This association is reinforced by the kneeling posture adopted by professional players, who traditionally play on free-standing boards placed on the floor, with piece stands for the captured pieces. Visually this is indeed the complete antithesis of sumo wrestling! Nevertheless, shogi is hugely popular and its top adherents are revered as glamorous figures with much higher profiles than their most of their western chess counterparts.

In the west shogi is still very much in its infancy, but official organisations have already sprung up in the United States, Holland, France, Belgium, Germany, Austria, Sweden and the UK.

Tournament Calendar

All tournaments are held annually and the season is considered to run from 1 April – 31 March (any year quoted refers to the year that a season began). Title holders must meet a challenger in a match and the preliminaries are run on a cycle that ensures that title matches are staggered throughout the year.

The most prestigious and now the richest title is the Ryu-O (created in 1988 to replace the Judan title). The winner receives 32 million yen (about £200,000) and the loser 8 million yen. Players are divided into six groups and a final stage of 11 players (four from group 1, two from group 2, two from group 3 and the winners of groups 4,5 & 6) sees a knock-out event with a best of three final to produce a challenger. The title match is best of seven played October-December. (There is always at least a week, usually two, between title games.) There is a complicated system of promotion and relegation between the groups.

Ryu-O Matches

Year	Players	Result
1999	Fujii Takeshi bt Suzuki Daisuke	4-1
2000	Fujii Takeshi bt Habu Yoshiharu	4-3
2001	Habu Yoshiharu bt Fujii Takeshi	4-1
2002	Habu Yoshiharu bt Fujii Takeshi	4-3
2003	Moriuchi Toshiyuki bt Habu Yoshiharu	4-0

For historical and other reasons the Meijin tournament holds a special place in the shogi world. The title was first contested in 1937 at the dawn of modern tournament shogi. All professionals are divided into five classes, A, B1, B2, C1 and C2, known as the Jun'i-sen tournament or Meijin leagues. This affects both their promotion and salary as well as determining their seeding in some other events.

Lifetime Meijins

In early shogi history the title of Meijin was reserved for the clearly outstanding player of the time. There were even times when two really great players were denied the title because neither could establish superiority. However, the rivalry between the shogi families of the Edo period often resulted in the succession being hereditary, the title passing to the Meijin's son or favourite pupil, usually an adopted son, who was not necessarily deserving of this honour.

In 1937 the 13th Meijin, Sekine, bequeathed the title of Meijin to the Nihon Shogi Renmei (the Shogi Federation) to be played for annually and thus modern tournament shogi was born. The Renmei continues to award the title of Lifetime Meijin to players with outstanding records. Below is the official list of Lifetime Meijins with the date they assumed the title: (Japanese names are given with surname first.)

	Player	Year
1	Ohashi Sokei I	1596-1615
2	Ohashi Soko	1634
3	Ito Sokan I	1654
4	Ohashi Sokei III	1691
5	Ito Soin I	1713
6	Ohashi Soyo II	1723
7	Ito Sokan II	1728
8	Ohashi Sokei VI	1789
9	Ohashi Soei I	1799
10	Ito Sokan III	1825
11	Ito Soin III	1879
12	Ono Gohei	1898
13	Sekine Kinjiro	1921
14	Kimura Yoshio	1952
15	Oyama Yasuharu	1976
16	Nakahara Makoto	after he retires
17	Tanigawa Koji	after he retires

The next player to win the Meijin title five times will become the 18th Lifetime Meijin. (Habu Yoshiharu has won it four times so far.)

The Greatest Modern Player?

Oyama Yasuharu was born on 13 March 1923 and became pupil of Kimi 8-dan in 1935. He first won the Meijin title from Kimura (the 14th Lifetime Meijin) in 1952 and dominated shogi from the early 1950's to the early 1970's. In all he contested 112 title matches of which he won 80: 18 Meijin, 20 Osho, 14 Judan, 12 Oi and 16 Kisei. He also won another 44 lesser tournaments. He became the 15th Lifetime Meijin in 1976 and died in 1992 while still an active player.

Shogi Records

Most Titles

Player	Titles
Oyama Yasuharu	80
Nakahara Makoto	64
Habu Yoshiharu	56
Tanigawa Koji	27
Yonenaga Kunio	19

Most Women's Titles

Shimuzi Ichiyo with 31.

Youngest Meijin

Tanigawa Koji at the age of 21 in 1983.

Youngest Title-Holder

Yashiki Nobuyuki at the age of 18 in 1990.

Youngest Title Challenger

Yashiki Nobuyuki at the age of 17 in 1989.

Youngest 4-Dans

Kato Hifumi at 14 years, eight months; Tanigawa Koji at 14 years, eight months; Habu Yoshiharu at 15 years, two months.

Oldest Meijin

Yonenaga Kunio at the age of 50 in 1993.

Oldest Meijin Challenger

Oyama Yasuharu at the age of 63 in 1986.

Oldest Title-Holder

Oyama Yasuharu at the age of 59 in 1982.

Oldest Title Challenger

Oyama Yasuharu at the age of 66 in 1989.

Lowest Ranked Title-Holder

Goda Masataka was a 4-dan in C2 when he won the 1992 Oi title.

Most Games in a Career

All time: Oyama Yasuharu – 2214.

Active players: Kato Hifumi – 2182.

Most Career Wins

All time: Oyama Yasuharu – 1433.

Active players: Nakahara Makoto – 1273.

Most Encounters between two players

All time: Nakahara Makoto 106-80 Yonenaga Kunio (+1 jishogi draw).

Active players: Habu Yoshiharu 80-58 Tanigawa Koji.

At the end of each season awards are given for most games played, most wins, best percentage score and most consecutive wins. (As most tournaments have a knock-out stage, playing a lot of games is prestigious as it implies success). The all-time records in each category are:

Most Games Played

Player	Games	Year
Habu Yoshiharu	89	2000
Yonenaga Kunio	88	1980
Tanigawa Koji	86	1985
Nakahara Makoto	82	1982
Habu Yoshiharu	80	1988
Moriuchi Toshiyuki	79	1991

Most Wins

Player	Wins	Year
Habu Yoshiharu	68	2000
Habu Yoshiharu	64	1988
Moriuchi Toshiyuki	63	1991
Habu Yoshiharu	61	1992
Kimura Kazuki	61	2001

Best Winning Percentage

Player	%	Year
Nakahara Makoto	85.5	1968
Habu Yoshiharu	83.6	1995
Kimura Kazuki	83.6	2001
Kiriyama Kiyosumi	82.6	1968
Nakahara Makoto	82.1	1966

Most Consecutive Wins

Player	Wins	Year
Kamiya Hiroshi	28	1986-87
Maruyama Tadahisa	24	1995
Tsukada Yasuaki	22	1986
Habu Yoshiharu	22	1992
Yamasaki Takayuki	22	2003

At the end of the 1995 season Habu Yoshiharu became the only player ever to hold all seven major titles simultaneously and, as a result of this, has been the only shogi player to merit a colour feature in *Time* magazine.

Now, some ten years later, he is down to one title, the fewest he has held in a decade.

Cross-cultural activity

Many shogi professionals are also strong go players, while Oyama in his day was one of the best Xiang Qi players in Japan. There has long been an awareness of Western chess and indeed Alekhine's 1933 win in a simultaneous display over Kimura, the 14th Lifetime Meijin, features in the 3rd volume of his selected games.

Recently, two of the top shogi professionals, Habu and Moriuchi, have made forays into Open chess tournaments in the US and France, and both achieved ratings over 2300 which, given their limited opportunity to play and study, is quite remarkable.

In 2002 Habu played an all-play-all in Paris, the 2nd NAO Masters and scored 50%. This tournament featured the first head-to-head encounter between a shogi title-holder and an ex-world Championship Candidate. The veteran Taimanov achieved a strategic triumph with the variation that bears his name, only to let his opponent escape with a draw at the last moment.

White: Yoshiharu Habu
Black: Mark Taimanov
NAO Masters, Paris 2002
Sicilian Defence

1 e4 c5 2 Nf3 e6 3 d4 cxd4 4 Nxd4 Nc6 5 Nc3 Qc7 6 g3 a6 7 Bg2 Nf6 8 0-0 d6 9 Be3 Be7 10 f4 0-0 11 Nb3 b5 12 a3 Bb7 13 g4 Nd7 14 g5 Nb6 15 Kh1 Nc4 16 Bc1 Rfd8 17 Qh5 g6 18 Qh3 b4 19 axb4 Nxb4 20 Nd4 Bf8 21 Nd1 e5 22 Nf2 exd4 23 Ng4 f5 24 Nf6+ Kh8 25 Ra4 d5 26 exf5 Bc8 27 Rxb4 Bxb4 28 Nxd5 Rxd5 29 Bxd5 Bb7 30 Qf3 Bxd5 31 Qxd5 Rd8 32 Qe6 gxf5 33 Rf3 Ne3 34 Qf6+ Kg8 35 g6 h6 36 c3 Bf8 37 Bxe3 dxe3 38 Rxe3 Qb7+ 39 Kg1 Rd1+ 40 Kf2 Qxb2+ 41 Re2 Qb3 42 Kg3 Qd5 43 Re3 Rg1+ 44 Kh4 Rg4+ 45 Kh5

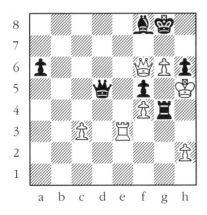

45 ... Rxf4?
45 ... Rg2! wins.
46 g7 Qf7+ 47 Qxf7+ Kxf7 48 gxf8Q+ Kxf8 49 Kxh6 Draw agreed

CHAPTER FIVE

XIANGQI (CHINESE CHESS)

Brief Description

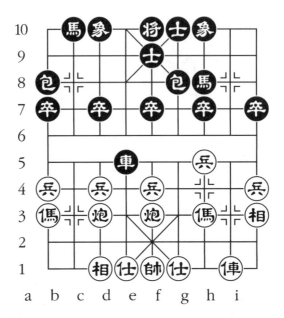

The object of xiangqi, as with shogi and western chess, is to checkmate your opponent's king. (A king is checkmated when no reply can get it out of check.) The side who forces the mate scores a win against his or her opponent. Unlike western chess, where a stalemate is a draw, one can also win in xiangqi by forcing your opponent into a position where there is no legal move. Also, like go but unlike chess or shogi, play is on the intersections rather than the squares (see illustration in plate section). In addition, you win if your opponent resigns or oversteps the time limit.

Chinese chess has more possible first moves than western chess. Double checks are extremely common during play, with occasional triple checks. In fact, it is possible to give quadruple checks in Chinese chess.

A high percentage of western chessplayers in China are actually xiangqi crossovers. Chess Grandmasters Xu Jun, and Ye JiangChuan were both at one time xiangqi hopefuls. Of course the most famous example is former Women's World Chess Champion Xie Jun, who was a junior xiangqi champion in Beijing.

The most popular opening is the Cannon Opening, in which Red (who goes first) moves a cannon to the central file, attacking Black's centre pawn. In theory, this gives Red a longer initiative than any other opening.

Historical Development

Origins

There are many similarities between xiangqi and its western cousin and this certainly suggests a common origin. Although, historically, the Chinese have always maintained xiangqi was locally invented, the prevailing theory on the origin of chess before the 1970's (which was largely based on H.J.R.Murray's work) favoured the so-called 'Indian Connection'. However, since the 1970's, more and more weight has been given to the idea that China already had a version of chess before India. This is an intriguing area of Mind Sports history, which requires further research, and, given the great antiquity of go, the Chinese may well have a valid prior claim.

There were mentions of the game 'xiangqi' in documents during the Warring States period (403-221BC) and even earlier. Chinese historians generally agree that the modern version was reached sometime during the late Tang Dynasty (AD618-906). This is supported by recent unearthing of ancient artefacts, with a xiangqi set identical to the modern set that dated back to the Song Dynasty. For a long period, xiangqi was snubbed by high officials, and the game of go was preferred by the higher classes. However, xiangqi, with its charms and characteristics, quickly became a game for the masses. From the Song Dynasty through the Qing Dynasty, the game began to be more accepted by officials, and numerous records were referenced in bureaucratic manuscripts and scholarly works.

The Modern Game

After the Qing Dynasty fell, both Nationalists and Communists had many devoted followers of the game. Both Dr Sun Yat-Sen (Sun YiXian by PinYin), Chiang Kai-Shek (Jiang JieShi by PinYin) and Mao Tse-Tung (Mao ZeDong by PinYin) were quite keen players, and Chou EnLai (Zhou EnLai by PinYin) was near master strength. From 1949 on, mainland China and other Asian regions all went through a great surge in xiangqi popularity, but in separate parallels. In 1956, the game was officially listed as a sports item in China and began its National Championship cycles. The same event also produced the first National Champion in the person of Yang Guan Lin, who almost single-handedly caused Guangzhou in Canton to be known as 'XiangQi City'.

During the infamous Cultural Revolution, xiangqi was banned, among many other things, while outside China it prospered. In 1968, the first of seven Asian Team Tournaments (the first two cycles were called 'Southeast Asian XiangQi Championships') was held in Singapore, helping to unite south-east Asian nations/regions.

The Advent of International Competition

1980 marked another historical milestone, as China finally joined the Asian XiangQi Federation and entered international competition, at the First Asian Cup Tournament held in Macao. The Chinese players quickly showed their dominance, and wrapped up every title that they contested. While China is the strongest xiangqi nation and Hu RongHua of Shanghai is recognised as the greatest player of all-time, there had never been a system to compete for and award the title of World Champion. Then the first World Cup Tournament was held in Singapore, in April 1990. Lu Qiu of China won the men's title, narrowly ahead of Hu, no longer in his prime. While the system is far from being perfect, the event did provide an answer to the question of who is the World Champion of xiangqi.

Currently China is the only place which has a rating system. Grandmaster and master titles have been awarded to players since 1982 and a national rating list is compiled twice a year.

The Greatest Player of All-Time?

Hu RongHua is generally regarded as the greatest player of all-time. His talent is unequalled and his record of winning the national title (it should be considered the world title in reality, in view of the dominance of the mainland players) ten times running will be nearly impossible to break. Hu single-handedly brought the ancient Bishop Opening and the Pseudo Two Knights' Defence back to life. He reached a peak in xiangqi that no one, past or present, has touched.

What the Future holds

XiangQi is extremely popular in nations like Vietnam, Malaysia, Thailand, etc. Since it is the most popular board game of the world's highest populated nation, plus the large percentage of Chinese immigrants over the world, xiangqi could well be the most played board game in the world, even surpassing western chess.

XiangQi has advantages over western chess as a spectator sport:

- For the same number of men, xiangqi has a much larger board (90 points vs. 64 squares, which is over 40% larger), which means more open positions, i.e. more tactical actions.
- It has a shorter time control (40 moves in 90 minutes at championship level), making it more appealing to the general audience.

There are, though, three reasons why xiangqi has not attained the worldwide popularity it deserves. First, it still suffers from political and bureaucratic influences that greatly hinder its international development. Though the recent political climate seems to have improved, no one is sure what the next round will bring.

Second, there has been as yet no serious effort on a large scale basis to promote the game worldwide. As its name implies, the Asian XiangQi Federation is mainly for Asian regions. Its officials appear to be content with the status quo of having a team event and an individual tournament every other year among a dozen members, and award a few individual titles (not based on ratings) once in a while. The Chinese XiangQi Association, under whose auspices 95% of all XiangQi literature is published, has yet to come up with a decent textbook in other languages. This lack of 'transfer of knowledge' is – and will be – the major stumbling block for foreign developing regions. The recently founded World XiangQi Federation (April 1993 at Beijing), brings hope. But at this time, no one can tell what changes it will bring forward, to truly globalise the game.

Third, although in the past xiangqi has been played with pictorial disks, showing the pieces, it is now universally conducted by means of Chinese ideograms. This makes it problematic for Western players to recognise the pieces.

XiangQi Stories

The Qing Dynasty's 'Last Emperor' FuYi, in his autobiography, recounted the true case of the Dowager Empress Tzu-Hsi (CiXi by PiuYin), who was very fond of the game. One day the Empress was playing one of the old servants. The servant said 'Your humble servant will take your Highness' horse', and the Empress broke into a sudden rage: 'Then I'll take your life!' And she ordered her opponent promptly beheaded.

Song Dynasty's first Emperor, Zhao, supposedly lost the mountain HuaShan as a wager on the result of a game of xiangqi to ChenChuan, a fairy-like figure. The opening that Chen used, the Pawn Opening still carries the nickname 'Fairy's Hand'.

Hu HanMin, a close associate of Dr Sun Yat-Sen and one of the most prominent figures in the founding of the People's Republic of China, died while playing xiangqi. In a winning position, Hu inadvertently let his rook be pinned in front of his king by his opponent's cannon. He promptly had a stroke and died.

XiangQi Records

Top Twenty Players of All-Time

The following current players (with ratings)

Rank	Player	Rating
1	Lu Qin (Guangdong)	2556
2	Zhao GuoRong (Heilongjiang)	2534
3	Hu RongHua (Hebei)	2510
4	Li LaiQun (Shanghai)	2524
5	Xu TianHong (Jiangsu)	2502
6	Liu DaHua (Hebei)	2468
7	Yu YouHua (Zhejiang)	2460
8	Lin HongMin (Shanghai)	2451
9	Xu YinChuan (Guangdon)	2437

plus Yu YouHua, Huang SongXuan, Li QhingQuan, Zhou DeYu, Xie XiaXun, Zhong Zhen, Jia TiTao and Zhang KuanYun – from the 1930's and 1940's, and Lee CheeHoi, He ShunAn, Chen SongShoon – from the 1950's and 1960's.

Youngest Champion

Hu RongHua, who won the national title at age 15 in 1960.

Youngest Women's Champion

Hu Ming, also at age 15 in 1986.

Oldest Champion

Hu RongHua won the title for the 12th time in 1985 aged 40.

Longest Sequence of Victories

Hu RongHua won every national singles title from 1960 to 1979 – 10 times running, spanning 20 years! Actually in 1962 he shared the title with Yang GuanLin, and there were no national events in the years 1961, 1963 and 1967 to 1972 (due to the Cultural Revolution), while the 1976 final was cancelled due to Chairman Mao's death.

2001 Brain Games Network Xiangqi Challenge

This World Xiangqi Challenge was staged in Beijing during 2001. It was a knockout event starting with 32 invited Chinese masters. Each two-day stage consisted of two games with a blitz finish decider if needed. During play from 18 April to 25 April, the 32 players were whittled down to 2. The two finallists, grandmasters Xu Yingchuang and Tao Hanming met on June 9, 15, 22 and 29 and then July 6 and 20. The games were televised to the whole of China and followed by thousands logged on to Globalink (www.ourgames.com). Xu Yingchuang of Guangdong won the final match 4½-1½ and took the first prize of 100,000 US dollars.

How Difficult are They?

The number of possible positions available in different Mind Sports is as follows:

Mind Sport	Possible Positions
Go	10^{170}
Scrabble	10^{150}
Poker	10^{72}
Shogi	10^{70}
Chess	10^{50}
XiangQi	10^{50}
Bridge	10^{30}
Draughts	10^{20}
Backgammon	10^{19}

CHAPTER SIX

GO

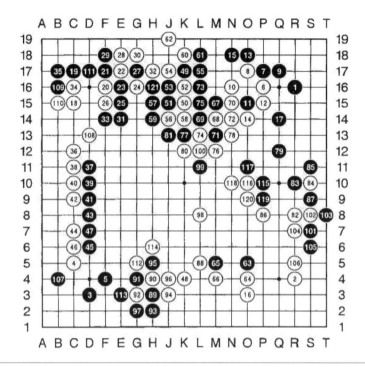

'Chess is humankind's greatest invention. Go, its greatest discovery...'

Chinese proverb

Brief Description

The Chinese game of go has been said to be an analogy for business management, Buddhist theory and warfare. (A book entitled *The Protracted Game* was published in the mid-1970s proving that Mao Tse-Tung's military campaigns were based on go strategy.) Go is about 4,000 years old. In China it is called *wei ch'i*, 'the surrounding game', but it reached Europe from Japan, and is therefore usually known here by its Japanese name.

It is a game for two players. Black and white pieces (stones) are placed alternately on the intersections of an initially empty 19 x 19 board (see diagram on next page). Victory goes to the player who ultimately controls more territory.

Historical Development

Origins

There are several legends about the origin of go. The most popular has it that the game was invented by the Chinese Emperor Shun 'to strengthen his son's weak mind'. Most players would certainly claim that go is mind-bending!

It is referred to in Chinese texts of about 1000BC as a game any reader would know. Yi Qiu was the first named go player in literature, being mentioned by Mencius in the 4th century BC, although the first book exclusively on go was not written until about AD700. Confucius is said to have known how to play, and traditionally the Four Sublime Pastimes were music, painting, calligraphy and go.

Growing Popularity and Military Training

Although it reached Japan around AD700, go was for centuries prohibited for the common people. It remained a privilege of the nobility and in particular the samurai, who regarded go as good military training, and even took it with them on campaign. The game achieved a peak of prestige in the 17th to 19th centuries, when it enjoyed the patronage of the shoguns. Four professional go academies were established, and there was great rivalry which culminated in the Castle Games. This was an annual match played in the presence of the shogun. Contestants were not allowed to leave the castle until the games were finished. The parallels with the development of shogi in Japan at that time are quite fascinating and reveal a society deeply absorbed by mental games.

Indeed, as early as the 16th century in Japan, both shogi and go came under the direction of a government department, the Ministry of Shrines and Temples. Both games were thought to be an adjunct of the Buddhist religion, possibly as a result of the attitudes of contemplation and meditation, common to these activities.

Go van Winkle

Legends, literature and art took go as a theme. The earliest known picture of go, showing a woman seated at the board, dates from around AD690, and was discovered during an archaeological excavation in China. The enduring cultural importance of go is clear from scores of Japanese prints, mostly 17th to 18th century, depicting gods and humans intent upon the game.

One legend still echoes in modern usage. A woodcutter in ancient China came upon two gods playing go in the mountains. He became so absorbed in watching the game that he was completely oblivious to the passage of time. When he came to his senses, he found that decades had passed, and the handle of his axe had crumbled away. The World Go Federation yearbook, printed in Tokyo (in English) is called *Ranka*, which means 'the crumbled handle'.

The Modern Game

After the fall of the shogunate in 1863, go lost its patronage and declined. However, in the 1890's fresh prosperity, as with shogi, came through newspaper sponsorship. There is now a professional body of over 400 players, a go column is a standard feature in many Japanese newspapers, and weekly lightning go contests are shown on TV. Major championships have first prizes of several hundred thousand dollars pounds a year, and several European and American experts have emigrated to Japan to seek their fortune in the rigorous world of the go professionals.

In 1968, an eight-storey go centre was built in Tokyo to accommodate national administration, professional competitions, facilities for TV coverage, and large playing areas. The influence of this go centre radiates far: in 1989 the first round of the Meijin Sen, or Grand Championship, was played in London. This event was sponsored by the newspaper group Asahi Shimbun International, which provided generously for British go players to attend the occasion, and have their own tournament.

Expand and Go

The most rapid expansion in the popularity of go has taken place in South Korea, where even the guidebooks refer to *baduk* as a game that most people play. (Interestingly the word 'Baidaq' was the Arabic word for a pawn in the old game of chess, popular in the Baghdad Caliphate in the 10th century.) Korean player Cho Chi-kun emigrated to Japan at the age of six. He swore that he would not go back to Korea until he won the title of Meijin (Supreme Grand Master). He had to wait 18 years, but in 1981 was able to visit Korea as a national hero, receiving a decoration from the President, a keen go player.

In China, go has flourished or wilted according to the political climate. Since 1974 it has been viewed as part of the national heritage and there is now an annual tournament between the top players of Japan and China. In Taiwan, too, go is thriving. Nearly every European country has a National Go Association affiliated to the European Go Federation. The European Go Congress, which lasts a fortnight, is hosted each year by a different country. There are now thousands of enthusiasts in the west, and it is a rapidly growing band. Many millions of people in the east enjoy go (there are estimated to be ten million regular club players in Japan alone). Edward Lasker, the well-known chess expert, wrote in *Go and Go-moku*: 'I am convinced that go will gradually share with chess the leading position among intellectual games in the Occident.'

The top twenty Chinese professionals now include four women of whom the strongest, Rui Naiwei, the world's only female 9-dan, reached the semi-finals of the 1992 Ing Cup World Championship. The strongest player now resident in Europe is another Chinese woman, Guo Juan, settled in Holland with a young family. Comparing the mathematics of chess and go games, we estimate that the number of possible positions in chess is 10 to the power of 50. For go, the estimate is 10 to the power of 170, a record amongst Mind Sports.

Poems, Legends and Anecdotes

Saying 'Just one game'
they began to play...
That was yesterday

Losing at go, when he returns, the house
becomes a tempest.

With an exalted person
playing go, and in danger of
winning, he thinks hard.

Last week I played the Chief Secretary of the Board of Rites and
won.
He advanced me one rank.
This week I lost.

He advanced me two ranks.
Does not victory lie in discretion?
Po Lien-yi (AD1043-1129)

A taoist adept passed through our village. He pontificated, 'Go is
like a conversation between two sages.'
After I lost all four corners I wondered If he were not doing too
much of the talking.
Po Lien-yi

Mountain monks sit playing go.
Over the board is the bamboo's lucent shade.
No one sees them through the glittering leaves, But now and then
is heard the click of a stone.
Po Chu-i (AD772-846)

But if you are too greedy to capture his stones, He will break
down your walls,
And when the dyke bursts it will not be stopped
But will overflow and the flood reach far and wide.
Ma Rong (Circa AD166)

Two friends used to play go every night until very late, oblivious to every-thing around them. One night a burglar sneaked in and filled his bag. Just as he was about to leave he heard the click of a go stone. Being a go player, his curiosity was aroused, and with his bag still slung over his shoulder he peeped through the doorway.

Gradually he moved in, until he was right beside the players. One player was about to make a move.

'That's no good!' the burglar exclaimed, putting down the bag. 'You ought to play on the other side.'

Both players were studying the board.

'Onlookers are supposed to keep quiet,' one of the men said. 'This happens to be a crucial moment in the game.' He glanced up briefly. 'Who might you be, anyway?' he asked and clicked a stone down on the board.

All three studied the move. It was a tense moment.

'I'm a burglar,' came the reply.

'Hmmm...' Click went another stone. 'I see...' Click. 'Well, make yourself at home.'

An event showing the courage of Sato Tadanobu (AD1160-1186) has become the most common subject among woodblock prints relating to go. One version of the story is that Tadanobu was taking a bath when his mistress Kaya (the word is also the name of the wood from which the best go boards are made) slipped away to alert enemy troops. Hearing the commotion of their arrival, he snatched up a kimono, and rushed out, to find that she had taken the precaution of hiding his sword. He picked up the first weapon he found, a *goban*. (This traditional oriental go board is a block of wood about six inches thick and weighing around thirty pounds, no slight weapon!) With it he scattered his opponents.

In the 18th century play *Gion Sairei Shinkoki Matsunaga Daizen*, the disloyal governor of Kyoto, who is involved in complicated plots to overthrow the Ashikaga Shogunate, is playing a game of go with his brother on the edge of the veranda in the Temple of the Golden Pavilion, and discussing their schemes. A stranger, bound with ropes, is led into the garden. A servant announces that he has just discovered him lurking outside the walls.

The stranger, really an Ashikaga loyalist, gives his name as Tokichi, and says he simply wants to enter Daizen's service. To test his brain power Daizen challenges him to a game of go. Tokichi wins the game and Daizen is annoyed. As a further test, he throws one of the go bowls into a well in the garden and commands Tokichi to retrieve it without getting his hands wet. Tokichi rises to the challenge with a brilliant stroke. He diverts a bamboo tube carrying water from a nearby waterfall into the garden, so that the water runs into the well, rapidly filling it and causing the bowl to float to the top. He scoops it up with his fan, places it on the go board, and ceremoniously presents it to Daizen. This time Daizen is delighted with Tokichi's quick wit and admits him into service, thereby setting himself up for destruction by the time the play ends.

Ignoring the Bomb

Although its go column had been suspended in March 1945, the *Mainichi* newspaper supported the third Honinbo title match. Iwamoto Kaoru, 7-dan, was the challenger to Hashimoto Utaro. Finding a venue in bombed-out Tokyo was impossible, but Kensaku Segoe came to the rescue; with the help of friends, he arranged for the match to be played in his hometown of Hiroshima. The players had been warned by the Hiroshima police chief not to play within the city, as it was too dangerous. They took advantage of his temporary absence to play the game as scheduled, on 23-25 July, ignoring the rain of bullets on the roof from strafing aeroplanes. Iwamoto won.

When the police chief heard on his return what they had done, he was furious and absolutely forbade them to play any more games in Hiroshima. It was arranged to play the second game in a house in Itsukaichi, an outer suburb of Hiroshima, on 4-6 August.

On the third day of the game, the players saw the Enola Gay fly in. Hashimoto later stepped out into the garden and saw the flash of the atomic bomb and the mushroom cloud rising above the city. A great blast of wind broke the windows, made a mess of the room and upset all the pieces, but since they had reached the endgame, they set the position up again and finished the game, which led to a five point win for Hashimoto. It was not until evening, when the streams of survivors pouring out of Hiroshima began to reach Itsukaichi, that they realised the magnitude of the disaster and just how lucky they had been. The house where they would have played was destroyed.

Both players survived into the 1990s and Hashimoto Utaro died in 1994.

The Go Player's Almanac, p.57-58. Ishi Press, Tokyo.

Go Records

Top Ten Players of All-Time

Rank	Player	Born	Age at Peak
1	Go Seigen	1914	35
2	Honinbo Shusaku	1829	33
3	Sakato Eio	1920	44
4	Kobayashi Koichi	1952	40
5	Honinbo Dosaku	1645	40
6	Cho Chikun	1956	37+
7	Rin KaiHo	1942	35
8	Honinbo Shuei	1852	50
9	Otake Hideo	1942	35
10	Fujisawa Hideyuki	1925	53

It is very difficult to obtain fair comparisons of players from different centuries and different countries. Players on this list from previous centuries would all have taken some time to catch up with modern theory, and they are here measured more by the extent of their pre-eminence among their contemporaries than any supposed match by time travel.

Top Ten Current Players

All the players listed rank as Professional 9-dan. There is a wide gap between amateur ratings and professional ratings in Japan. Unless otherwise stated, all references are to professional ratings.

Rank	Player	Born	Birthplace/resident
1	Kobayashi Koichi	1952	Japan/Japan
2	Cho Chikun	1956	S. Korea/Japan
3	Rin Kai Ho	1942	China/Japan
4	Nie WeiPing	1952	China/China
5	Yamashiro Hiroshi	1958	Japan/Japan
6	Cho Hun-hyun	1953	S. Korea/S. Korea
7	Lee Chang-ho	1975	S. Korea/S. Korea
8	Takemiya Masaki	1951	Japan/Japan
9	Ma XiaoChun	1964	China/China
10	Otake Hideo	1942	Japan/Japan

World Champions

(World Championships have only been held in the last few years, but, in practice, there is no single recognised championship, rather a series of top title tournaments.)

Samsung Cup

1996 Yoda Norimoto   1999 Lee ChangHo   2002 Cho Hun-hyeon

1997 Lee ChangHo   2000 Yu Ch'ang-hyeok   2003 Cho Hun-hyeon

1999 Lee ChangHo   2001 Cho Hun-hyeon   2004 Cho Chikun

Chinese CCTV

1990 Qian Yupimg	1995 Ma Xiaochun	2000 Ding Wei
1991 Ma Xiaochun	1996 Cao Dayuan	2001 Hu Yaoyu
1992 Ma Xiaochun	1997 Nie Weiping	2002 Ma Xiaochun
1993 Nie Weiping	1998 Cao Dayuan	2003 Zhou Heyang
1994 Ma Xiaochun	1999 Chang Hao	2004 Gu Li

Mingren

1990 Ma Xiaochun	1995 Ma Xiaochun	2000 Ma Xiaochun
1991 Ma Xiaochun	1996 Ma Xiaochun	2001 Ma Xiaochun
1992 Ma Xiaochun	1997 Ma Xiaochun	2002 Zhou Heyang
1993 Ma Xiaochun	1998 Ma Xiaochun	2003 Qiu Jun
1994 Ma Xiaochun	1999 Ma Xiaochun	2004 Qiu Jun

Tianyuan

1990 Liu Xiaoguang	1995 Ma Xiaochun	2000 Chang Hao
1991 Nie Weiping	1996 Ma Xiaochun	2001 Chang Hao
1992 Nie Weiping	1997 Chang Hao	2002 Huang Yizhong
1993 Liu Xiaoguang	1998 Chang Hao	2003 Gu Li
1994 Ma Xiaochun	1999 Chang Hao	

Japanese Kisei

1990 Kobayashi Koichi	1995 Kobayashi Satoru	2000 O Rissei
1991 Kobayashi Koichi	1996 Cho Chikun	2001 O Rissei
1992 Kobayashi Koichi	1997 Cho Chikun	2002 O Rissei
1993 Kobayashi Koichi	1998 Cho Chikun	2003 Yamashita Keigo
1994 Cho Chikun	1999 Cho Chikun	2004 Hane Naoki

Meijin

1990 Kobayashi Koichi	1995 Takemiya Masaki	2000 Yoda Norimoto
1991 Kobayashi Koichi	1996 Cho Chikun	2001 Yoda Norimoto
1992 Kobayashi Koichi	1997 Cho Chikun	2002 Yoda Norimoto
1992 Kobayashi Koichi	1998 Cho Chikun	2003 Yoda Norimoto
1994 Kobayashi Koichi	1999 Cho Chikun	

Honinbo

1990 Cho Chikun	1995 Cho Chikun	2000 O Meien
1991 Cho Chikun	1996 Cho Chikun	2001 O Meien
1992 Cho Chikun	1997 Cho Chikun	2002 Kato Masao
1993 Cho Chikun	1998 Cho Chikun	2003 Cho U
1994 Cho Chikun	1999 Cho Sonjin	

Korean LG Petroleum Cup

1996 Yu Ch'ang-hyeok	1999 Seo Pong-su	2002 Lee Sedol
1997 Lee ChangHo	2000 Ch'oe Myeong-hun	2003 Lee ChangHo
1998 Lee ChangHo	2001 Lee ChangHo	

Wangwi

1990 Cho Hunhyun	1995 Yoo Changhyuk	2000 Lee Changho
1991 Lee Changho	1996 Lee Changho	2001 Lee Changho
1992 Yoo Changhyuk	1997 Lee Changho	2002 Lee Changho
1993 Yoo Changhyuk	1998 Lee Changho	2003 Lee Changho
1994 Yoo Changhyuk	1999 Lee Changho	2004 Lee Changho

Guksu

1990 Lee ChangHo	1995 Lee ChangHo	2000 Cho Hunhyun
1991 Cho Hunhyun	1996 Lee ChangHo	2001 Lee ChangHo
1992 Cho Hunhyun	1997 Lee ChangHo	2002 Lee ChangHo
1993 Lee ChangHo	1998 Cho Hunhyun	2003 Choi CheolHan
1994 Lee ChangHo	1999 Rui Naiwei	

Youngest World Champion

Lee Chang-ho won the Tongyang Securities (South Korea) World Championship at the age of 17 in 1992.

Oldest Title-Holder

Fujisawa Shuko won a title at 66 years of age and again at 67. He is the oldest player to win a major Japanese tournament.

Oldest Player to reach 9-Dan

Nakamura Yutaro won promotion to 9-dan at the age of 73 in 1981.

Most Invincible Player

Shusaku: won all 18 of the official Castle Games in his career.

Most Consecutive Tournament Wins

Takagawa Shukaku won the Honinbo Tournament for nine successive terms between 1952-1960.

Longest Career

Sakata Eio, a professional for 55 years, recorded his 1,000th win in 1986.

Longest Winning Streak

29 by Sataka Eio. Since there is a one in two chance of winning a game, the odds of winning 29 in a row are said to be 500 million to one. Sakata Eio achieved this while embroiled in top title matches.

Longest Session

Hoshino Toshi and Suzuki Goro played for six days without sleep in 1933.

Most Games Played Simultaneously

Shirae Haruhiko played 154 games simultaneously in Japan in 1994.

First Western Professional Tournament Winner

James Kerwin became the first Westerner to enter the record books of professional tournament go when he won the 1-dan section of the fourth Kisei Tournament in 1978.

First Westerner to beat a Professional in a World Championship

Rob van Zeijst became the first western amateur to defeat a professional at the 1996 Samsung event, where he beat a Korean 6-dan.

Richest Tournament

Ing Chang-Ki established the richest go tournament ever in 1988 with first place prize money of US$400,000. The Samsung tournament also now has a $400,000 prize.

Youngest winner of an open title

Cho Chikun won the Pro Best Ten title aged 18, in 1975.

Shortest professional game

In 1996 Kudo Norio 9-dan defeated Ono Nobuyuki 6-dan in 20 moves. Ono resigned when he realised that he had misread a sequence.

Longest professional game

In 1950 Hoshino Toshi 3-dan defeated Yamabe Toshiro 5-dan taking 411 moves. He won by two points.

Most games played simultaneously

Shirae Haruhiko played 154 games simultaneously in Japan, in 1994.

Bad Omen

Oda Nobunaga was the first of the three great Japanese warlords who ended centuries of chaos and provided Japan with an effective central government at the end of the sixteenth century. On June 1, 1582, while staying in the Honnoji monastery in Kyoto, he is said to have watched a game between the leading Go player, Nikkai, and Kashio Rigen, in which a triple ko occurred and the game had to be abandoned. That night one of Nobunaga's own generals, Akechi Mitsuhide, surrounded and attacked the monastery, and Nobunaga was killed.

A triple ko is now regarded as a bad omen. Some attribute this to the occurence of one soon before the betrayal of Nobunaga. Others believe that the incident is mythical, and was invented to explain why triple ko is a bad omen.

CHAPTER SEVEN

DRAUGHTS/CHECKERS

'Playing chess is like looking out over a limitless ocean; playing checkers is like looking into a bottomless well.'

Dr Marion Tinsley (World Champion 1955-1958 and 1975-1991)

Brief Description

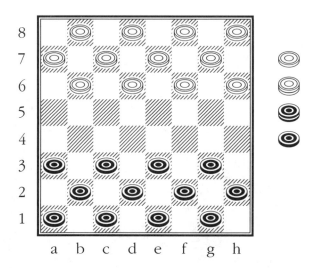

Draughts (British), also called checkers (North American), is played by two opponents facing each other over a board of 64 squares, with Black moving first. The board is arranged with the bottom corner black square on the player's left. All play is conducted on the black squares only. The above diagram shows the pieces set up for play. The object of the game is to capture all of the opponent's men, or render them unable to move.

Historical Development

Origins

Draughts lovers would have us believe that a game similar to draughts may have been played in Egypt as far back as 1600BC. Part of a board and pieces were discovered in the tomb of Queen Hatshepsut, daughter of Thothmes the first, who ruled Egypt for many years. There is evidence too, from Egyptian monumental paintings and inscriptions, that the game was common at the time of the earlier pharaohs. In the *Dialogues of Plato*, Socrates tells Phaedrus that the famous Egyptian god Theuth '... was the inventor of many arts, such as arithmetic and calculation and geometry and astronomy and draughts and dice, but his great discovery was the use of letters.' Homer, in his *First Book of the Odyssey*, says: 'The blue-eyed goddess Athene ... found the insolent suitors, sitting on the hides of oxen that they had taken and slaughtered themselves, playing at draughts.' Of course, the use of 'draughts' in this context may be the whim of a modern translator, but illustrations from Ancient Greece (such as the famous 'Vatican vase') certainly show a board game, similar in appearance to draughts, being played.

Naturally, as we point out in our chapter on backgammon, this illustration, and others like it from Egyptian and Classical antiquity, may equally well refer to ancient race-style games. Indeed, it is quite common for draughts sets to include 15 pieces on each side (rather than the required twelve) simply so that they may double as backgammon counters.

The Modern Game

Modern draughts may be said to have had its beginnings in Spain, with the publications of Anton Torquemada in 1547, Pedro Rodrigo Montero in 1590, Lorenzo Valls in 1597 and Juan Garcia Canlejas in 1610. In France, Pierre Mallet, Mathematician to the King, published a manual in 1688 entitled *Jeu des Dames*. Confident of his ability and knowledge of the game, Monsieur Mallet challenged any Christian or Barbarian Champion to play a match for a dozen pistoles.

The pioneer of draughts literature in England was William Payne, a teacher of mathematics, who published his *Treatise on the Game of Draughts* in 1756. The book contained 50 games, 'Critical Situations', 'Situations for Strokes', and many fundamental endgame positions, including an analysis of 'First Position', by which more games are won than any other ending. The book revealed that even two and a half centuries ago, the experts of the day knew a great deal about draughts.

Another valuable contribution to the literature of the game was made by the publication in 1800 of a work by Joshua Sturges, entitled *Guide to the Game of Draughts*, which contained a great deal of original analysis and corrected faulty play in Payne's book. Sturges' book went through many editions, and furnished a foundation for later analyses. Other publications in the next half-century worthy of particular intention include James Sinclair's *Game of Draughts* (1832), William Hay's *The Game of Draughts* (1838) and John Drummond's *The Scottish Draughts Player* (also 1838). However, the most important contribution to the science of the game during that period was that of Andrew Anderson of Carluke, Scotland, one of the greatest players that ever lived and one of its most skilled analysts. His work, *The Game of Draughts Simplified* (titled thus by some, and by others Anderson's *Guide to the Game of*

Draughts), was published in 1848 and enlarged in 1852. Anderson's book offered a great deal of dependable analysis (it was rare indeed that a flaw could be found in an Andersonian line of play). This book also provided a set of 'Standard Rules for Play', and a naming of the basic openings.

As an analyst, Anderson was unrivalled, and as a player – well, he beat the mighty James Wyllie in four matches out of five they played. Andrew Anderson was the first man ever to be recognised as World Champion, largely by his victory over James Wyllie in 1847 in a match for the title. He scored nine wins to six losses, with 31 games drawn. According to some sources (for example *Bishop's Encyclopaedia of Checkers*) Anderson's tenure as World Champion actually dates from 1840.

Different 'Styles' of Play

Three 'styles' of play are contested at the World Championship level. 'Go-as-you-please' (GAYP), also known as free-style, is the name given to the style in which each player has complete freedom as to his or her opening moves, from the very first move of the game. Because so many opening variations are known to lead to a draw, GAYP lacks popularity at the top echelons because many players would not want their opponents to be able to make an easy draw.

To reduce the number of draws, in 1894 the convention was adopted that the first move for each player was randomly determined (by the draw of a card, or ballot). Since some of the opening lines were advantageous for one of the sides, for each opening selected two games would be played; each player getting a chance to play with the black pieces. So-called 'two-move ballot' draughts forced players to study more openings, increasing the variety of play and reducing the number of draws.

The strong players quickly mastered the opening intricacies of 'two-move ballot'. The logical extension was to go to 'three-move ballot', and this happened in 1934. There are 174 possible 3-move sequences (ignoring move transpositions), of which 156 are sanctioned for tournament play. The remained 18 openings are barred from tournament play; typically, the opening line results in one side immediately losing a checker. Three-move ballot is used in all major tournaments and for world championship matches.

'Eleven-man-ballot' is another way of spicing up the game. There are several variations on this theme, but a commonly used variant is where each player starts with 11 men instead of 12 and the first two moves for each side are pre-determined. The locations of the missing pieces and the initial two moves are chosen by ballot.

Dr Marion Tinsley: The Greatest Mind Sportsman of Them All?

Dr Marion Tinsley was born in 1927. He is universally recognised as the premier draughts player in the history of the game. Tinsley was winner of a record seven US National titles. He first won the three-move ballot World Championship in 1955, but retired in 1958 to further pursue his teaching career in mathematics as a professor at Florida State University. Returning to the game in 1970, his 12-year absence seemed to be no obstacle, winning the 1970 US National Title and earning the right to play for the World Championship. The World Champion, Walter Hellman, was ill, so Tinsley declined to play the match and retired again. He returned to active play in 1975 and won the World Championship, which he maintained until he retired (again!) in 1991. In 1992, Tinsley was declared World Champion Emeritus in recognition of his outstanding record. Over the period 1950 to 1991, Tinsley lost fewer than 10 serious games of draughts – a feat unrivalled in the history of professional sport. Tinsley died in 1995.

Man vs. Machine

> *'Chinook has an excellent programmer in Dr Jonathan Schaeffer, but mine is better – God!'*
> Dr Marion Tinsley, on the occasion of his 1992 match against the Chinook computer.

IBM researcher Arthur Samuel wrote the first competitive draughts program in the 1950s. The program was a vehicle for his pioneering work in machine intelligence. Samuel's program played a competent game of draughts, occasionally defeating good players. The highlight of the program's career was playing 4-game exhibition matches against World Championship combatants Walter Hellman and Derek Oldbury in 1966 – mankind won all 8 games.

A serious electronic challenger for the best players did not emerge until 1990, when the draughts program Chinook (Dr Jonathan Schaeffer from the University of Alberta) caused a stir by coming second to Tinsley in the US National Championship. Tinsley and Chinook battled each other in four games – all exciting draws. By coming second to the incumbent, Chinook earned the right to challenge Tinsley for the World Championship.

In 1992 Tinsley faced his greatest ever challenge – a forty-game contest against Chinook for the World Man-Machine Championship. This historic clash, organised by the co-authors and International Chess Master David Levy, was the first between a human World Champion and a computer program aspirant to the throne. The match attracted more widespread media coverage than any other modern draughts contest.

Tinsley prevailed in what was arguably the finest high-level draughts match ever played, by the score of four wins to two with 33 draws. The final game of the match had the packed hall enthralled as the advantage swung from Chinook's side to Dr Tinsley. After the game was over, Dr Tinsley said that this had been the most exciting match of his entire career. According to the many watching draughts experts, the standard of play was possibly the highest ever seen in a draughts match.

By 1994 Schaeffer's team was ready for the rematch, having improved both the computing software and hardware used by Chinook. Again Tinsley enthusiastically accepted the challenge. Obviously ill and suffering from abdominal pains, Tinsley held his opponent to six draws before being told to stop by his doctor. (He was later diagnosed as having advanced cancer of the pancreas and died in April 1995.) Tinsley thus conceded the world title to Chinook, creating a landmark in the history of Mind Sports, the first ever computer World Champion.

Chinook defended its Man-Machine title in two subsequent matches. After winning the 1996 US National Championship by the unprecedented margin of 8 points (out of 32), the program retired. Man could not compete successfully against machine any more. Today, there are at least half a dozen computer programs that play draughts at a super-human level.

Perfection at Checkers

Since 1989, the Chinook team has been building databases of solved endgame positions. In early 1995, they completed building the collection of all positions with 10 or fewer pieces on the board – roughly 39,000,000,000,000 (39 million million) positions. For each position, the program knows the final win, loss, draw result. Using these databases, the Chinook team announced in January 2005 that one of the most challenging of all checkers openings, the so-called White Doctor, has been proven to be a draw. That means Chinook will never lose a game played with this opening – and might win if the opponent makes a mistake. There are 173 openings remaining to be solved, but only about 50 need to solved to prove the value of the standard starting position in checkers (presumably a draw). This historic event will happen in the next few years.

Draughts Records

Top Ten Human Players of All-Time

	Player (country)
1	Marion Tinsley (USA)
2	Richard Jordan (Scotland)
3	Walter Hellman (USA)
4	Samuel Gonotsky (USA)
5	Asa Long (USA)
6	James Wyllie (Scotland)
7	Robert Yates (USA)
8	Robert Stewart (Scotland)
9	Willie Ryan (USA)
10	Newell Banks (USA)

It is interesting to note that no current players are on this list.

World Champions (Men)

Player (country)	Dates	Style
Andrew Anderson (Scotland)	1840-1844 [1]	GAYP
James Wyllie (Scotland)	1844-1847	GAYP
Andrew Anderson (Scotland)	1847-1849	GAYP
Robert Martins (England)	1859-1864	GAYP
James Wyllie (Scotland)	1864-1876	GAYP
Robert Yates (USA)	1876-1878 [1]	GAYP
James Wyllie (Scotland)	1878-1894	GAYP
James Ferrie (Scotland)	1894-1896	GAYP
Richard Jordan (Scotland)	1896-1903 [1]	2-Move
Alfred Jordan (England)	1912-1917	2-Move
Newell Banks, (USA)	1917-1922	2-Move
Robert Stewart (Scotland)	1922-1933 [2]	2-Move
Newell Banks (USA)	1933-1934	2-Move
Asa Long (USA)	1934-1948	3-Move
Walter Hellman (USA)	1948-1955	3-Move
Marion Tinsley (USA)	1955-1958 [1]	3-Move
Walter Hellman (USA)	1958-1975 [2]	3-Move
Marion Tinsley (USA)	1975-1991 [1]	3-Move
Derek Oldbury (England)	1991-1994 [3]	3-Move
Ronald King (Barbados)	1994-2002	3-Move
Alex Moiseyev (USA)	2002-present	3-Move

NOTE:
[1] Retired as champion.
[2] Forfeited title on doctor's orders.
[3] Passed away as champion

World Champions (Women)

Player (nationality)	Dates	Style
Joan Caws (England)	1986-1993	3-Move
Patricia Breen (England)	1993-	3-Move

Youngest World Champion

Robert Yates (USA) at the age of 19.

Youngest Female World Champion

Patricia Breen (Ireland) at the age of age 16.

Youngest American Champion

In 1922, Asa Long wins the US National Championship at the age of 18.

Oldest American Champion

In 1984, Asa Long celebrated his 80th(!) birthday by winning the US National Championship.

Youngest English Champion

Sammy Cohen at the age of 18.

Oldest World Champion

James Wyllie at the age of 66.

Longest Sequence of Victories

Dr Marion Tinsley played in seven USA National tournaments from 1954 onwards (1954, 1956, 1970, 1978, 1982, 1990) winning each one – without ever losing a single game! He was internationally undefeated in match play from 1947 until his death in 1995.

Simultaneous Marathon World Record

Charles Walker played a record 306 in a simultaneous display at Dollywood, Pigeon Force, Tennessee, USA in October 1994, losing just one.

Blindfold Marathon World Record

In 1947 Newell Banks (USA) played draughts while blindfolded four hours a day for 45 consecutive days, winning 1,331 games, drawing 54 games, while losing just two games! Furthermore, he was playing six games simultaneously throughout.

Record Winning Margin

In November 1996, world man versus machine champion Chinook scored 30/32 in the US Championship at Danville, Virginia, finishing a record eight points ahead of the number two player, Ron King. Chinook, though, did not win the US title since it was only permitted to play hors concours.

Longest Game

The longest games of draughts on record are two games consisting of 210 moves each. One was the 55th game of the Championship of England and Scotland in 1867 between Robert Martins and James Wyllie, resulting in a won game for Martins. The second was a match game between Robert Yates and James Wyllie held in 1876, which resulted in a win for Wyllie.

CHAPTER EIGHT

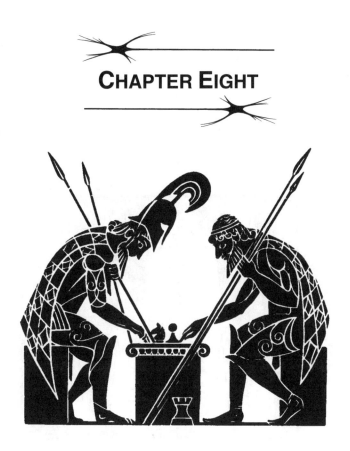

BACKGAMMON

Brief Description

Backgammon is a game that takes five minutes to learn and a lifetime to master. The board, with its 24 triangular points, is familiar to most, because it is traditionally found on the reverse of the draughts board in a games compendium. You need 30 checkers to play, 15 of each colour, two dice and if you are going to progress beyond the beginner stage, a doubling cube, the six faces of which have the numbers 2, 4, 8, 16, 32 and 64. The starting position is shown in the diagram.

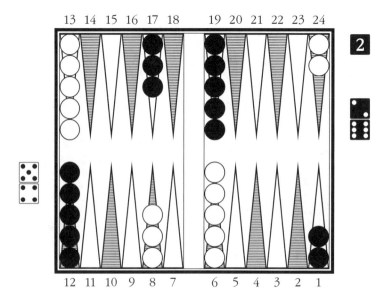

Backgammon is basically a race game and the players move the pieces round the board according to the dice rolls, each player rolling two dice on his turn. White is moving his pieces anti-clockwise, until they are all in his home board, which is the segment of six (1-6) points in the bottom right hand corner. Black is moving clockwise towards her home board in the top right corner (19-24). Once a player has all his men in the home board, he may begin to bear them off the board with his rolls. The first player to bear off all his men wins. Two simple rules introduce the complications that provide the game with its interest. When a player has two or more checkers on a point, he holds that point and his opponent cannot land there. For example, in the above diagram, White can't play a 5 with one of the checkers from the top right hand corner. This means that creating blocking points, particularly against the two checkers that start on the 24 point, is an essential strategy.

Also, a single checker on a point (known as a blot) is vulnerable to being hit, that is his opponent may, if he rolls the right number to land on that point, hit the checker and send it off the board, from where it has to re-enter and start again. This means that a player far behind in the race can still turn a game around with a lucky hit late in the game. This isn't quite enough information to start you playing, but any board that you buy will contain the few and simple rules that you need to know.

Historical Development

The earliest known backgammon boards are thought to be those found at Ur, in present day Iraq, during the excavation of Sumerian tombs by Sir Leonard Woolley in the 1930's. They date from about 2,000 BC. The game spread all over the world, being particularly popular in the Persian, Greek and Roman empires and there are references to it in the writings of Plato and Sophocles. Chaucer refers to it in his Canterbury Tales and it was so popular during the reign of Henry VIII that cardinal Wolsey issued an edict requiring all boards to be burned! A board from this period was found in the hull of the King's flagship, sunk in 1545 and raised from the seabed in 1971. Both board and ship are on display in the Mary Rose museum in Portsmouth.

Edmund Hoyle published *A Short Treatise on the Game of Back-gammon* in 1745 and it shows a fairly sophisticated understanding of probabilities and strategy. Three point matches were the norm and the game was often played for enormous stakes. In America, the game became very popular in 1920's high society and about this time, an unsung genius invented the doubling cube. This device allows a player, before any turn, to double the stakes. His opponent may either resign the game, paying the single stake, or play on for double. The accurate assessment of winning chances that this requires, gives the modern game much of its interest. The rules were standardized in New York in 1931 and a number of textbooks date from then. There was another, more widely based, surge of interest in the 1970's, coinciding with the first reasoned analysis of what constituted good play. Established experts such as Oswald Jacoby and Barclay Cooke inspired a younger generation to think about the game, in particular the young Paul Magriel. His *Backgammon* is a truly great book, still in print and still relevant for all learners today. From this flowed the work of the theoreticians on which all modern players base their game, most notably perhaps Bill Robertie, Danny Kleinman and Kit Woolsey.

From America, the game has spread all over the world and many smaller countries now rival the USA in expertise, particularly the Scandinavian countries and Germany. Theoretical development is now driven by computer programs, the best of which, based on neural net technology, are now stronger than all but a handful of players. Thousands of players play online on real-time servers, for fun and for money.

The Modern Day Game

Today the game is played all over the world, but it doesn't have a properly constituted governing body, although several individuals have organizations with 'World' in their title. However there is a flourishing tournament scene on national and international levels. The most famous tournament is The World Championships held in Monte Carlo every year since 1979. This attracts fields of about 300 players in the top division, competing for a prize fund of around 250,000 euros and the prestige of the title. The Nordic Open in Denmark every Easter is the most popular European event and in the USA, the largest tournaments are those held in Las Vegas.

There is no universal rating list as in chess. The top players don't meet often enough for it to be particularly relevant and the ideal system for rating a game with such a large luck element has yet to be devised. However players vote bi-annually for the Giant 32 and with their matches now so widely available for study and analysis, this produces a reasonable list of the best.

The Top Ten

Rank	Player	Country
1	Nack Ballard	USA
2	Jerry Grandell	Sweden
3	Dirk Schiemann	Germany
4	Johannes Levermann	Germany
5	Paul 'X-22' Magriel	USA
6	David Wells	USA
7	Neil Kazaross	USA
8	Mike 'Falafel' Natanzon	Israel
9	Mads Andersen	Denamrk
10	Jorgen Granstedt	Sweden

The World Championship with its sudden death knock-out format is not ideally suited to produce the best player of the year and many great players have never won, but the title does carry significant prestige. Three players are two-time winners: Bill Robertie (USA) in 1983 and 1987, Michael Meyburg (Germany) in 1991 and 1998 and Jorgen Granstedt (Sweden) in 1999 and 2001. Jerry Grandell (Sweden) and Peter Jes Thomsen (Denmark) have also been losing finalists in addition to their win, while the unfortunate Thomas Holm (Denmark) has achieved the unenviable feat of being the losing finalist in successive years. Not many women feature at the top level, but they have had their champions, most recently Katie Scalamandre (USA) in 2000 and Norway's Katja Spillum reached the semi-final in 2003, after being European champion in the preceding year.

There are hundreds of useful web-sites with information about the game, all of which can be reached through Art Grater's Portal at www.back-gammon.com.

The best online magazine is Gammon Village at www.gammonvillage.com , subscription with some free content and the best play sites are at www.fibs.com, a free site and www.gamesgrid.com, a pay site but where guests are welcome.

The best first book to buy is unquestionably *Backgammon* by Paul Magriel, essential reading to understand the principles and subtlety of this beautiful game.

The best PC programs, to play against and learn from, are Snowie 4 Pro from Oasya, (www.bgsnowie.com), strong but expensive and Gnu, available as a free download at www.gnubg.org

The combination of luck and skill in this ancient and beautiful game, means that the novice can often win in the short run, even against an expert. This makes it an easy game to get into and the players tend to be sociable and friendly. It can be enjoyed on any level, but those who revel in mental stimulation can look forward to endless avenues of delight in backgammon, always varied and never to be mastered.

CHAPTER NINE

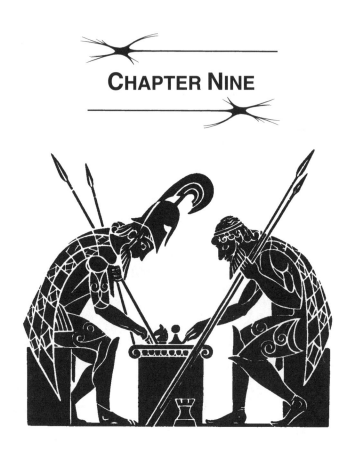

BRIDGE

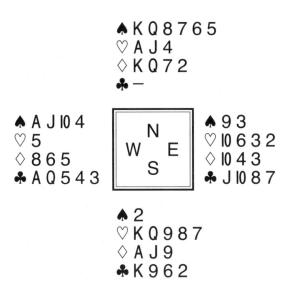

Brief Description

Bridge involves four players using a standard pack of cards (without jokers). Cards rank A, K ... 2 (low). For the bidding only, suits rank, in descending order, spades, hearts, diamonds and clubs, but a call in no trumps has precedence over spades.

Partners are agreed and face each other across the table. Each partnership works as a team but the bids of each partner are binding on both. The aim is to win the most points in play, especially by succeeding in contractual bids and so earning a bonus for winning games and for winning the rubber (best of three games). A slightly different system is used in tournaments, to eliminate luck.

Historical Development

Origins: The Father of Bridge

Harold Vanderbilt (1884-1970) known as the 'Commodore', had many distinctions. He was born into the richest and most famous American family of the times and lived a life cushioned by the fortunes of the family railroad business. He successfully defended the America's Cup three times and his revision of the right-of-way rules for sailing vessels are still known as the Vanderbilt Rules.

But his lasting fame derives from an experiment conducted in 1925 while cruising from Los Angeles to Havana via the Panama Canal. Together with three friends he tinkered with the rules of the two most currently fashionable card games of the whist family, known as auction bridge and plafond. Whist-type games had been played for 400 years or more, and had experienced several refinements in a slow evolution. What Vanderbilt did was alter the scoring in two critical details, by the introduction of slam bonuses and of the concept of vulnerability. He called his new version contract bridge and with only one very minor change in the 70 years that have passed since then, his is the version now played throughout the world and known simply as bridge.

His scoring system was so balanced as to make every aggressive or sacrifice bid an approximately even bet, allowing just enough difference to permit the exercise of fine judgement. Never mind that millions of people play bridge every day, sublimely indifferent to mathematical subtlety and happily oblivious of the arithmetical absurdity of most of their bids and plays. One of the game's abiding attractions is that it can be played and enjoyed by the merest amateur with little skill and no money staked, or fought out at the highest levels in silent intensity with large sums of money riding on the finest calculations. Vanderbilt's game achieved instant popularity. Remarkably, most of the basic bidding tools in use worldwide today were invented either by him or in the first ten years of contract bridge. He himself thought up the strong club, the weak diamond response, the strong no trump and the weak opening two. Other essential weapons in today's arsenal are the Stayman convention (late 1920s), the Lightner double (1929), Blackwood (1933), the suit preference signal (1934) and the Josephine grand slam force (1936). The high-low signal, without which a bridge player is crippled, had already been invented, by the whist-playing Lord Henry Bentinck in 1834.

The Modern Game

All inventions need popularising and the extraordinary and immediate growth of bridge was largely due to one of the strangest and most flamboyant characters ever known in the games-playing world. Ely Culbertson (1891-1955) was born in Romania and educated in Russia and at many universities (Yale, Cornell, the Sorbonne and the University of Geneva) without apparently getting any degrees. But he spoke fluent Russian, English, French, German, Czech, Spanish and Italian and had a reading knowledge of Slavonic, Polish, Swedish and Norwegian, as well as classical Latin and Greek.

He engaged in revolutionary activities in Russia, Mexico and Spain, but had to turn to card-playing to make a living when the Russian Revolution of 1917 wiped out the family's large fortunes. The new game of contract bridge provided him with the opportunity to build an empire. In the winter of 1931-

1932 he challenged his leading rival Sidney Lenz to the 'Bridge Battle of the Century', offering odds of five to one. No-one foresaw the passionate interest that this would arouse. Clearly, for the card-playing American public, enthusiasm had graduated into mania.

They played 150 rubbers – Culbertson won by 77-73 playing mostly with his wife Josephine – which is about 75 hours of play. The second half of the match took place in the newly opened Waldorf Astoria and the whole event was the first ever to be fully recorded and analysed. Individual deals were reported on the front pages of all important American newspapers. The Culbertsons' success enriched them mightily: he and his wife were contracted to write widely syndicated newspaper articles, he received $3,601,000 for a series of short movies and an amazing $10,000 a week for radio broadcasts.

Spreading like Wildfire

In only a few years since the Commodore's cruise, bridge had arrived. Today it is the world's most widely played card game. There are perhaps 17 million players or more in the United States, maybe as many as 250,000 in the UK.

Nearly 100 countries compete in the World Championships. The Epson computer company organises an annual pairs contest in which more than 100,000 people play the same bridge hands simultaneously all over the world. Using the internet, obsessive bridge players can set up a game, between four people who have never met each other and who may live in different corners of the world, and play against each other on the screens.

The Personality

Culbertson was the game's first great character. *The Official Encyclopaedia of Bridge* records that he lived in a grand manner 'with total disregard of expense whether at the moment he happened to be rich or penniless. Once he strolled into a Fifth Avenue store and bought $5,000 worth of shirts. He smoked a private blend of cigarettes that cost him $7 a day.'

But he took his card-playing very seriously, spending much of the time pacing the floor and thinking. When a reporter asked him how he got to be better than other players, he replied: 'I got up in the morning and went to work.'

In the two generations that have passed since then, some of the sharpest minds in the world have delved into the game of bridge, devising the best bidding systems and the best way of playing all possible card combinations.

The Fascination of the Game

Two specific elements in bridge make it unique in the entire world of games, intellectual or physical. The first of them derives from the astronomical numbers involved when a set of 52 cards is divided into four sub-sets of 13 cards each. The number of possible bridge deals is 10 to the power of 30. To describe each one of these in the bidding process, the players are allowed a vocabulary of precisely 15 words and a range of only 35 bids. It is hardly surprising that even the very best players occasionally find themselves in catastrophic contracts! Immensely complicated bidding systems have been devised, where the initial bids may have as many as five different meanings but opponents can always chip in, using up the bidding space and interfering with communications, much as in the military use of electronic counter-measures. One can even make out a logical case that every bid in bridge is a failure, because it further limits an already prohibitively inadequate situation!

The second unique element is that bridge is exclusively a doubles game. One can set up forms of one-against-one bridge events, for example sets of problems where an individual has to identify the best line of play, but in principle and practice bridge is always a contest between two pairs. This puts an enormous value on partnership understanding, tolerance and co-operation, still the area of greatest weakness, wherever the game is played. Two sound players in a trusting partnership are likely to defeat two quarrelsome prima donnas, even if the prima donnas are individually more skilled. Nothing is as valuable as partnership harmony. It is notable that poker players, probably the most mathematically acute of all card players, generally make bad bridge players. Poker players are remorseless individualists; they stare aghast and incredulous when informed they must have a partner and that the player sitting opposite them is actually on their side...

Finely balanced decisions are the stuff of life to keen bridge players, past and present: to the investor Warren Buffet, for instance, once rated the richest man in America by *Forbes* magazine; to the late President Eisenhower, commander-in-chief of the greatest army ever assembled; to the chess champions Lasker and Capablanca, who were early contributing editors to *The Bridge World*; to the former Chinese leader Deng XiaoPing who said: 'When the people see me swimming they know that I am physically fit and when they hear of me playing bridge they know I am mentally fit.'

Glamour

Bridge invades all worlds. You can find it in the works of Ian Fleming, Agatha Christie and Somerset Maugham. Harold Pinter plays the occasional game.

London's exclusive Portland Club includes as members Sir Rocco Forte, and the Earl of Carnarvon, the queen's racing manager.

Omar Sharif is a world-class player who has put together international teams and staged exhibition matches in many different countries. But Sharif was not the first great player from the film world. That honour belongs to the late Helen Sobel, rated by some as the best ever woman player. She once had a small part in the Marx Brothers' classic film *Animal Crackers*, and this was no accident. The Marx Brothers were keen bridge players and Chico is credited with one of the best systems ever devised: 'If you like my lead, don't bother to signal with a high card. Just smile and nod your head.'

Bill Gates, the second richest person ($34.2 billion) in the world from the software company he founded, *Microsoft,* regularly plays bridge. He enjoys playing computer bridge and rubber bridge. He has also played some National and International bridge. He played in the Mixed BAM Teams in 2000 where he qualified for the final. He played with Sharon Osberg in the World mixed Mixed Pairs in Montreal in 2002.

There is bigger money in poker, maybe in backgammon and definitely in gin rummy and Mah-jong, but in a high-stake, high-level bridge game one can lose £10,000 in a session. TGR's Club in London hosts some of the best and most expensive games anywhere. We once asked its then manager, British international Irving Rose [1938–96], how much a weak player might lose in a bad year, if he didn't have the wit to stop playing. 'Maybe £100,000,' he replied.

Passion

But the game is also a ritual, a social device, to meet people in a friendly but structured setting. Here is a definitive statement by an English financial analyst, a keen but, on his own admission, poor player. 'Bridge is not what you think. It is almost like a metaphor for life. Some years ago I was invited to make up a four and found myself partnering a woman I had not met before.

We were engaged the next day and married as soon as was decent. Anyone who tells you that bridge is only a game doesn't know what he's talking about.'

The (anti-)social dimension of the game also made its fateful appearance almost as soon as the game was born. Bridge's first tragedy occurred in Kansas City in 1931 when John Bennett, a perfume salesman, played a 'friendly' game with his wife against their neighbours, the Hoffmans.

Late in the evening he played a hand so badly that a furious row started between him and his wife. The Hoffmans' embarrassment turned to terror when Mrs Bennett left the room, fetched a pistol and shot her husband dead. The interest aroused was such that Culbertson himself was asked to analyse the hand. Mrs Bennett was later tried for murder but acquitted. They take their bridge seriously in Kansas.

Bridge Records

Biggest Tournament

The Epson World Bridge Championship, held on 20 and 21 June 1992, was contested by more than 102,000 players, playing the same hands at more than 2,000 centres worldwide.

Most Hands

In the 1989 Bermuda Bowl in Perth, Australia, Marcelo Branco and Gabriel Chagas (both Brazil) played a record 752 out of a possible 784 boards.

Most World Titles

The Open World Championship (Bermuda Bowl) has been staged from 1950 to 2003. The USA has won a record 15 times and are the current holders with Dick Freeman, Bob Hamman, Jeff Meckstroth, Nick Nickell, Eric Rodwell and Paul Soloway.

The British team won in 1955 with Leslie Dodds, Kenneth Konstam, Adam Meredith, Jordanis Pavlides, Terence Reese and Boris Schapiro.

The World Teams Olympiad has been staged from 1960 to 2004. The current Italian team has brought their country's Olympiad tally to six and they are the current holders with Norberto Bocchi, Giorgio Duboin, Fulvio Fantoni, Lorenzo Lauria, Claudio Nunes and Alfredo Versace.

Italy's Blue Team (Squadra Azzura) won 13 world titles and three Olympiads between 1957 and 1975. Giorgio Belladonna (1923-1995) was in all the Italian winning teams and his 16 world titles keep him at the top of the world list followed by other members of the Squadra Azzura.

The Bermuda Bowl, World Team Olympiad and the World Pairs comprise the international calendar. Only eight open players have won the triple crown: Marcelo Branco (Brazil), Gabriel Chagas (Brazil), Bob Hamman (USA), Pierre Jais (France 1913-1988), Jeff Meckstroth (USA), Eric Rodwell (USA), Roger Trezel (France 1918-1986) and Bobby Wolff (USA).

The Women's World Championship (Venice Bowl) has been staged from 1974 to 2003. The USA has a record nine wins. They are the current holders with Jill Blanchard-Levin, Betty Ann Kennedy, Janice Seamon-Molson, Sue Picus, Tobi Sokolow and Katherine Wei-Sender.

British teams won in 1981 with Sally Brock, Pat Davies, Maureen Dennison, Nicola Gardener, Sandra Landy and Diana Williams, and 1985 with Sally Brock, Michelle Brunner, Pat Davies, Nicola Gardener, Sandra Landy and Gillian Scott-Jones.

The Women's Olympiad has been staged from 1960 to 2004. The USA has a record five wins. Russia currently holds the title with its first bridge gold medal: Olga Galaktionova, Victoria Gromova, Natalia Karpenko, Maria Lebedeva, Tatiana Ponomareva and Irina Vasilkova.

The British team won in 1964 with Dimmie Fleming, Fritzi Gordon, Rixi Markus, Mary Moss, Jane Priday and Dorothy Shanahan.

There are seven triple crown winners all from the USA: Mary Jane Farrell, Marilyn Johnson, Betty Ann Kennedy, Jacqui Mitchell, Judi Radin, Carol Sanders and Kathie Wei-Sender.

The World Junior Championship has been staged from 1987 to 2003. Great Britain, Italy and the USA have each won on two occasions. Italy is the current holder of the title with Furio Di Bello, Stelio Di Bello, Ruggiero Guariglia, Fabio Lo Presti, Francesco Mazzadi and Stefano Uccello.

The British team in 1989 was John Hobson, Derek Patterson, John Pottage, Andrew Robson, Gerald Tredinnick and Stuart Tredinnick and in 1995 Jeffrey Allerton, Danny Davies, Jason Hackett, Justin Hackett, Philip Souter and Tom Townsend.

The World Individual Championships has been staged from 1992 to 2004. Noberto Bocchi of Italy holds the open title and Tobi Sokolow of the USA, the women's title.

Most Master Points

The World Bridge Federation awards Master Points based on performance in International Championships. Players who have sufficient points and have won at least one world championships are categorised as *World Grand Masters*. There are 56 players with this title. In the latest ranking list the leading Open players are:

Rank	Player	Country	Master Points
1	Lorenzo Lauria	Italy	3927
2	Giorgio Duboin	Italy	3860
3	Alfredo Versace	Italy	3818
4	Norberto Bocchi	Italy	3592
5	Robert Hamman	USA	3488
6	Jeff Meckstroth	USA	3460

The second category is *World Life master* with 132 members. Britain's highest placed player is Robert Sheehan in 82nd place with 138 MPs

50 women players hold the title *World Grand master* the leading players are:

Rank	Player	Country	Master Points
1	Jill Meyers	USA	2729
2	Sabine Auken	Germany	2715
3	Bep Vriend	Netherlands	2664
4	Tobi Sokolow	USA	2571
5	Shawn Quinn	USA	2430
6	Catherine D'Ovidio	France	2368

The highest placed British player is Nicola Smith in 18th place with 1570 MPs.

CHAPTER TEN

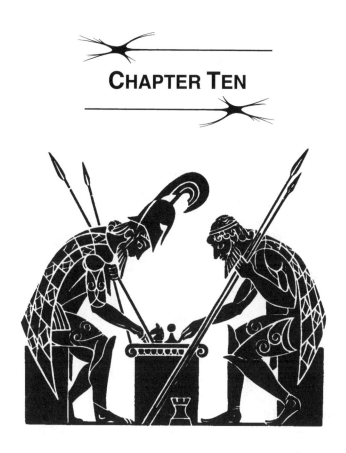

NUMERICAL AND VERBAL
CHALLENGES

Great Mental Calculators

William Klein (b. 1912)

In Rhode Island in 1982, aged 70, he multiplied two five digit numbers (57,825 x 13,489) together mentally in 42 seconds.

Shakuntala Devi

On the 18th June 1980, at Imperial College, London, she multiplied together two 13 digit numbers in 28 seconds:

7,686,369,774,870 x 2,465,099,745,779

(The answer: 18,947,668,177,995,426,462,773,730)

Mrs Devi also extracted the 23rd root of a 201 digit number in 50 seconds at the Southern Methodist University in Dallas, USA.

Truman Henry Salford (b. 1836)

In 1846, in Middletown, Connecticut, he calculated two 15 digit numbers in his head in not more than one minute:

365,365,365,365,365 x 365,365,365,365,365

And he correctly recited the answer from left to right:

133,491,850,208,566,925,016,658,299,941,583,225

R.H.Frost (b. 1931)

Calculation of adding a column of 100 digits. Achieved this feat in York University in 1977 in a best time (from five attempts) of 32.57 seconds.

Johann Martin Zacharias Dase (b. 1824)

In April 1847, Dase was reported as having achieved the following calculations: multiplying two 20 digit numbers in six minutes, two 48 digit numbers in 40 minutes, and incredibly two 100 digit numbers together in 8¾ hours (all these calculations performed mentally).

Additionally, 2 x 8 digit numbers: 49,735,827 x 98,536,474 in one minute and seven seconds on paper.

(Answer: 4,900,793,024,053,998)

However, mentally he was even quicker with: 79,532,853 x 93,758,479 in 54 seconds. (Answer: 7,456,879,327,810,587)

Zerah Colburn (b. 1840)

Demonstrated the mental multiplication of powers at the age of eight (1848 in London but born in Vermont, USA). For example, raised 8 to the 16th power, the answer being: 241,474,976,710,656.

Thomas Fuller (b. circa 1810)

In 1879 in Virginia, USA when he was about 79 years old calculated mentally the number of seconds elapsed in any given time period. For example, for 70 years, 17 days and 12 hours the correct answer was given in one and a half minutes: 2,210,500,800 (assuming a 365¼ day year).

Mirat Arikan (b. 1973)

In 1996 in Istanbul, Turkey, he calculated the 39th root of an arbitrarily chosen 100 digit number in 39 seconds.

Tathagat Avtar Tulsi (b. 1988)

Tulsi, a nine-year-old boy from a poor suburb Delhi, is being hailed as one of the world's greatest ever mathematical prodigies after working out the theoretical existence of a new sub-atomic particle, which he has christened the 'Tulitron'. Furthermore, Tathagat's claims that he calculated the value of pi to seven decimal places (3.1415927) at the age of six, have been backed up by testimonials from Indian scientists and physicians. His house, which he shares with his parents and two brothers, is crammed full of books, providing him with a unique environment in which to develop his ambitions of testing the Tulitron theory in a particle accelerator and ultimately to win a Nobel Prize.

Crossword Puzzles

Word-squares and puzzles have existed since the birth of Christ and opinions differ on how a true crossword differs from other word puzzles. However, there is little doubt that the modern puzzle evolved from Arthur Wynne's diamond-shaped 'Word Cross' published in the New York World on 21 December 1913.

Wynne thought his brainchild 'just another puzzle' but it immediately became a weekly feature and he worked with enthusiastic readers to develop the 'cross-word'. It soon became the symmetrical, mainly square design we see today. His paper remained the only one to use crosswords until 1924 when two Harvard graduates published a collection of its puzzles. Within the year, over 400,000 copies were sold and the publishing firm of Simon and Schuster was established.

Crossword mania erupted and, in London, The Times reported: 'All America has succumbed to the crossword.' A man shot his wife when she would not help with his crossword. Doctors gave a warning of 'a risk of developing neurotic traits through frustration' and of 'crossword patterns damaging the sight'.

Largest Published Crossword

Robert Turcot of Quebec, Canada, compiled a crossword with 82,951 squares in July 1982. It contained 12,489 clues across and 13,125 down and covered an area of 3.55 square metres.

Fastest Crossword Solver

The record for completing The Times crossword under test conditions is 3 minutes 45 seconds, by Roy Dean of Kent in December 1970.

National Crossword Championships

Between 1972 and 1990 Dr John Sykes won *The Times*/Collins Dictionaries championship ten times, solving the four puzzles in an average time of eight minutes each. He set a championship best of 4 minutes 28 seconds in 1989.

Scrabble

Scrabble – the world's leading proprietary word game – is played on a 15x15 board, more than a quarter of which carry premium values. There are 98 letters in the form of tiles that fit the squares. Each letter is marked with a value in rough inverse proportion to its frequency in the language: A, E, L and T are typical one point letters; Q and Z are ten point letters. Two blank tiles, acting as wild cards, complete the set.

The object of the game is to form words that score as many points as possible.

Scrabble was not simply invented overnight. It took nearly 20 years before its popularity took off to the phenomenal levels it has reached today. Over 100 million games have now been sold in 120 countries around the world and Scrabble is produced in 31 languages.

World Scrabble Champions

1991 Peter Morris (USA); 1993 Mark Nyman (England); 1995 David Boys (Canada)

Most National Championships

Philip Nelkon (b. 21 July 1956) has won the British Championship a record four times, in 1978, 1981, 1990 and 1992.

Youngest National Champion

Allan Saldanha, who won the British title in 1993, aged 15.

Highest Word Score

The highest ever word score acquired in a competition is 392 points by Dr Karl Khoshnaw from Twickenham in April 1992. To make this incredible score he spelt *caziques* which is the plural for a West Indian chief.

Highest Game Score

The highest ever game score is 1049 by Phil Appleby (b. 9 December 1957) in June 1989. His opponent scored 253 and the margin of victory, 796 points, is also a record. His score included a single turn of 374 for the word *oxidizers*.

Sudoku

A fresh mental challenge that has swept the UK is Sukoku – a fiendish number square challenge which can be traced back thousands of years to ancient Egypt but which has also been popular in Japan. One of the paintings by the German renaissance artist Durer depicts a magic number square highly similar to a Sudoku grid.

The puzzle is a 9×9 grid made up of 3×3 subgrids. Some cells already contain numbers, known as 'givens'. The goal is to fill in the empty cells, one number in each, so that each column, row, and region contains the numbers 1 through 9 exactly once.

The attraction of the puzzle is that the rules are simple, yet the line of reasoning required to reach the completion may be difficult. Published puzzles often are ranked in terms of difficulty. This also may be expressed by giving an estimated solution time. While, generally speaking, the greater the number of givens, the easier the solution, the opposite is not necessarily true. The true difficulty of the puzzle depends upon how easy it is to logically determine subsequent numbers.

The Times newspaper introduced the puzzle to the British public and were closely followed by all other major newspapers in running a daily puzzle. *The Times* sold out the entire 100,000 print run of their first Sudoku book within a week. Now *The Times* are organising the first ever British Sudoku Championships. These will take place at the Cheltenham Literary Festival in October 2005.

Carbon Calculation Power

Computers are becoming ever faster, larger in terms of storage capacity and yet smaller in physical size. However, we should not forget that the most remarkable computer ever to come into existence is the ultimately portable model that we are fortunate enough to carry around with us wherever we go.

Any computer scientist would cheerfully admit that a cockroach navigating its way across a kitchen floor exhibits substantially more carbon-based computing power than the most powerful silicon equivalent yet constructed.

Despite having access to trillions of bits of information and having the ability to process these at a rate of many millions per second, the silicon cockroach would be more likely to get trodden on than to arrive safely at its destination. Even if it negotiated this task, finding and consuming food to stay alive would represent an information processing hurdle that would make putting a man on the moon seem simple in comparison.

CHAPTER ELEVEN

WHO IS THE ALL-TIME GREATEST MIND SPORTS CHAMPION?

The automatic answer to the question of who is the greatest mind sports champion of allt-ime would be Garry Kasparov, undisputed number one for over twenty years, international media personality and multi-millionaire. However, Kasparov somewhat blotted his copybook by losing a six-game challenge match, in May 1997, to IBM's Deep Blue computer and also losing his world title to Vladimir Kramnik in London 2000. Meanwhile, draughts champion Dr Marion Tinsley made such a huge impression during his match in London against the Chinook program in 1992, that this question is definitely worth asking. For example, the implacable Dr Tinsley, aged 65, played four games a day (totalling nine hours), six days a week with only one rest day over a 39 game match.

Spectacularly, in so doing, Dr Tinsley turned the 'Turing Test' on its head. The Turing Test, famously, posits that if experts cannot distinguish between human and computer output in certain areas, then the machine is said to be 'thinking'. When analysts were poring over the 39 games played, they found to their surprise, that not knowing whether the human or the computer was playing black or white, they consistently concluded that the mistake-prone, relatively non-elegant moves played by the computer were those played by Dr Tinsley, while the magnificently immaculate moves played by Dr Tinsley were, in fact, by the computer. This provides a fascinating insight into how the human brain still underestimates itself and inappropriately overestimates silicon intelligence when the evidence is quite demonstrably to the contrary.

When seeking to answer the enthralling question, who is the greatest Mind Sports champion of all-time, a number of significant factors must be taken into account. Before we enumerate the critical criteria for establishing the greatest Mind Sportsman of all-time, we must be certain that we have selected the leading candidates from the major Mind Sports. Apart from Kasparov and Dr Tinsley the following five grand champions in their sphere should be considered:

Oyama Yasuharu

Oyama Yasuharu totally dominated the game of shogi for a twenty year period from the early 1950's to the early 1970's. He won 80 titles, overwhelmingly the largest number ever, and was still a title challenger in 1989 at the age of 66. He was created 15th lifetime Meijin (or grand champion) in 1976 and died in 1992 at the age of 69. This was in his 45th consecutive season as either an 'A' class player or as Meijin. In chess, this would be the equivalent of being World Champion, or a World Championship candidate, for 45 years. Additionally, he holds the record for the most number of games player in a career, 2,214 and the most career wins, 1,433.

Go Seigen

Go Seigen was the strongest player in the oriental game of go from 1940 to 1955. Born in Fukien Province, China, he emigrated to Japan and vanquished all the Japanese Grand Champions in a series of set matches. Go experts regard him as the greatest genius in the history of their game. Go Seigen achieved one of the dreams of all Mind Sports champions, in that he defeated every major opponent who confronted him on even terms. This forced them into a situation where they could only hope to compete against him with a chance of success while being given odds. Not just a great player, he was also a revolutionary theorist of the openings, developing the New Fuseki, which completely overturned conventional theory in go during the 1930's.

Hu RongHua

Hu RongHua won the XiangQi Championship for the first time in 1960 aged 15, thus creating the record for the youngest ever champion in that Mind Sport. In 1985, at the age of 40, he added the record for becoming the oldest champion too! Absolutely the greatest player of Chinese chess of all-time, Hu RongHua logged an unprecedented sequence of ten consecutive victories in the championship during his dominant years. The best Chinese chess players come exclusively from mainland China, and the Chinese National Championship may safely be considered as equivalent to the World Championship.

Ely Culbertson

Contract bridge was invented in 1925, but within the space of a mere six years bridge fever had swept America. The extraordinary and immediate growth of the game was largely due to Culbertson, one of the strangest and most flamboyant characters ever known in the games-playing world. In 1929 he founded the magazine *The Bridge World,* which is still a leading authority. His many textbooks became best-sellers and he commanded an amazing $10,000 a week for radio broadcasts on the game. In 1930 he led an American team to England to play the first ever international match. Culbertson won the 'Bridge Battle of the Century' in a 75-hour contest against Sidney Lenz in 1931. This success made Culbertson a dollar millionaire three times over. He went on to establish a sort of private fiefdom over bridge, which has never been equalled. Culbertson, like Kasparov, transformed success at his chosen Mind Sport into giant personal wealth. He lived on a private estate in a 45-room house, with several miles of parks, lighted roads, greenhouses, cottages, lakes and an enclosed swimming pool. He always had caviar for tea!

Dominic O'Brien

Dominic O'Brien is the overwhelmingly dominant force in the Mind Sport of memory testing and performance. He has been joint winner of the Brain of the Year title, awarded by the Brain Trust Charity, and has won the World Memory Championship on eight occasions.

Now we enumerate the criteria for awarding the ultimate laurels.

Criteria for establishing Dominance in Mind Sports

1 The number of players playing the particular game.

2 The strength of the top players.

3 The complexity of the game.

4 The record of the player in question.

5 The duration of time at the top.

6 The opinions of those who are the champions' closest rivals.

In spite of their superlative achievements, none of Hu RongHua, Culbertson, Oyama Yasuharu or Go Seigen ever faced the test of extended battle against a giant, tireless number-crunching computer, as Kasparov and Tinsley did. While, in Dominic O'Brien's chosen sphere of memory challenge, contests against a computer would simply be inappropriate. We must therefore narrow the field down to Kasparov and Dr Tinsley.

When assessing the relative claims of Kasparov and Dr Tinsley it should be noticed that there are more draughts players in the world (500 million) than there are chessplayers (350 million). However, there is a distinctly higher number of top chessplayers, and chess certainly has the lead in terms of the quantity of young players taking up the game as a profession. As to the relative complexity of chess and draughts, chess according to our research, has 11 skill levels, while draughts has 8, a clear lead to chess. Kasparov has dominated chess as no other player ever has, and has continually put his title on the line to challengers, but Dr Tinsley essentially maintained himself at the top, dominating all aspects of the game, including knowledge, opening, middlegame and endgame theory, brilliance, creativity, speed and marathon playing for a total of 43 years. If Kasparov had ambitions to duplicate Tinsley's span as the undisputed top player, he would have had to stay world champion until the year 2028 and he would have had to improve his record against the world's best computers!

CHAPTER TWELVE

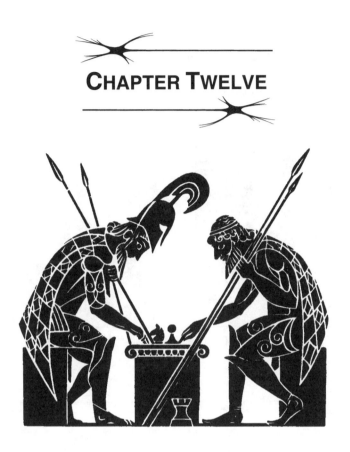

PUZZLES

In this chapter we choose challenging mental exercises for you, covering key areas of this book. The puzzles include: chess problems based on games by the youngest ever Grandmaster Sergei Karjakin, the world's strongest female chessplayer Judith Polgar, the mighty Hydra Computer and the greatest ever chessplayer Garry Kasparov and draughts positions selected by Dr Marion Tinsley. Finally, test your IQ and your Sudoku-solving abilities.

Chess

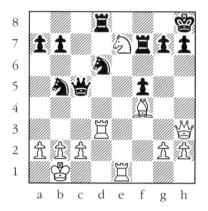

Puzzle 1: White to Play

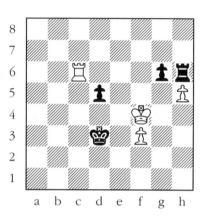

Puzzle 3: Black to Play

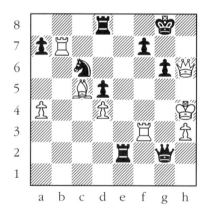

Puzzle 2: White to Play

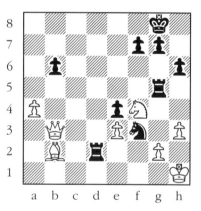

Puzzle 4: Black to Play

Puzzle 1

This position is from the game Karjakin-Metsalu, Tallinn 2001. Sergei Karjakin astonished the chess world by becoming an international grandmaster at the age of 12 years and 7 months. How did he finish off his opponent here?

Puzzle 2

This position is from Polgar-Hansen, Vejstrup 1989. Judit Polgar has maintained a position in the world's top twenty for nearly a decade. This makes her – by a considerable margin – the best woman player ever. Here she found a way to force a quick checkmate. Can you see the winning continuation?

Puzzle 3

This position is from the game Adams-HYDRA, London 2005. The Hydra computer has raised the bar for the performance of chess-playing computer programs with its astonishing 5½-½ win against Britiain's Michael Adams in London 2005. Adams has been ranked one of the world's top half dozen players for many years. Adams has already resigned in this particular game. What blow had he foreseen?

Puzzle 4

This position is a variation from Sunye Neto-Kasparov, Graz 1981. Garry Kasparov, who announced his retirement from competitive chess early in 2005 is, by common consent, the greatest player ever. This position features one of his most creative combinations. How can Black force checkmate?

Draughts

(White is playing up the board in both cases)

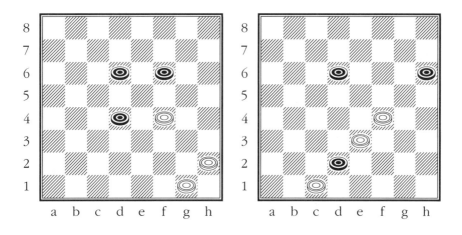

1. White to move and win   2. White to move and win

IQ

1. Which is the odd one out?

Salmon, whale, shark, trout, pike

2. Insert the two missing numbers:

6   9   18   21   42   45   ??   ??

3. Which is the odd one out?

Venus, Saturn, Hermes, Pluto, Uranus

4. Choose the word to complete the sentence:

Hearing is to acoustics as seeing is to ????????

5. Complete the row of numbers:

3   5   8   13   22   ??

6. Who is the odd one out?

Haydn, Mahler, Aristotle, Brahms, Stravinsky

7. Which is the odd one out?

Paris, Washington, Oslo, Cairo, Bombay, Rio de Janeiro, Berlin

8. Which is the odd number out?

625   361   256   197   144

9. Insert the missing letter:

B   E   ?   Q   Z

10. Complete the following number sequence:

4   6   9   13

7   10   15   ??

Sudoku

To solve the puzzle complete all the empty squares such that each row, column and 3x3 grid contains the numbers 1-9.

		5				3		
	2		7	5			4	
7				8	9			2
	4		2			9		
	8	6		9			5	7
		7			4		8	
6			9	2				8
	7			4	5		1	
		8				7		

Solutions on
page 159

CONCLUSION

The Cloud Of Unknowing

Part of the thrill of any sport is uncertainty as to the outcome and the relishing of the infinity of possibilities in play which have rendered many situations virtually impervious to definitive solution or accurate prediction – mental sports, specifically, fall into three categories:

1) Opponents battle against each other with the objective of winning, scoring points, achieving ratings and earning titles; chess, draughts, bridge and go, for example, fall into this category. In such games the truth – in an objective fashion – often falls victim to the overriding imperative to win the game.

2) Competitors battle against themselves, seeking to overcome their own limitations whilst maximising their personal potential to claw ever improving results out of the granite of set standards and norms. Such activities, always competitive but involving rivals rather than opponents, include – notably – Memory Championships, where the target is invariably to surpass previous records and shatter known barriers.

3) Finally we come to those mental activities, often highly testing, and again fiercely competitive, but where the challenge is to rediscover what is already known, perhaps in a race with other contestants against a time limit or clock. The competitions which fall into this category include crossword solving, IQ tests and chess problem solution. Ipso facto, the setter of the questions, problems or puzzles already knows the answer. The trick for the winners is to penetrate the mind of the composer and divine the intentions behind a query to which the answer is already established.

The Blurring Of The Lines

In recent times a particular technological phenomenon has caused variants 1 and 3 to veer much more closely towards each other. The advent of super-computers, such as IBM's Deep Blue, Fritz and now the monstrous Hydra, has created a situation where games such as chess, draughts and to a lesser extent Go can be analysed out to a correct conclusion, once the basic tactical and strategic environment has been adumbrated by the chosen opening moves. So strong have such programs become – with High Street devices on sale for a few tens of dollars able to defeat masters and on occasion grand-masters of the games concerned – that we are rapidly reaching a situation where a chess or checkers game may be seen as an examination rather than a pure combat. The players produce their moves, a result is obtained and then the analysts switch on the machines to discover who was right, who went wrong and where, and what the result should have been. The experience of contesting such a game now is beginning to resemble an examination with right and wrong answers, rather than a work of art or a battle.

How to React?

It has been established by impeccable scientific research that playing chess and dancing are the two sovereign remedies against Alzheimer's Disease and any general deterioration of mental faculties. However, it is also well established that any strenuous mental activity will assist the brain in cultivating new connections and perhaps even growing further cell tissue.

Hence mental sports and the striving for fresh mental records is an indisputably good thing, whether one battles against an opponent, oneself or an objective norm. That said, the possible transformation of face to face mind warfare of type 1 into a more objective testing of the type 3 variety, should not overly concern us.

What the leading practitioners must do, and in this sense all they have to demonstrate is the way forward for other enthusiasts, is to learn from computers, to draw and publish detailed conclusions when they fail to win or even lose. This occurred with Kasparov in 1997 against Deep Blue and more emphatically when Britain's number one Michael Adams was crushed by Hydra in 2005. After such reverses analysis must be produced, both strategic and tactical to show how losing positions came about and how they are to be avoided. If necessary copy machine stratagems and employ them in reverse against the machines themselves. This way the frontiers of knowledge will be advanced and the human brain will demonstrate that in the mental sphere miracles can be achieved.

In the Olympic games Formula One racing cars are, of course, not permitted to enter the 5000 metres or the marathon, but in the mental sphere computers are allowed to do just that. It is within the parameters of both the duty and the capability of the best mental warriors to prove that they can still survive in such an intense competive environment, digest the lessons to be learnt and go on to win.

Solutions to Puzzles

Chess

Puzzle 1) 1 Qxh7+! Kxh7 2 Rh3 mate.

Puzzle 2) 1 Qg7+! Kxg7 2 Rxf7+ Kg8 3 Rg7+ Kh8 4 Rh7+ Kg8 5 Rbg7 mate.

Puzzle 3) 1 ... g5+ wins the white rook.

Puzzle 4) 1 ... Rdxg2!! 2 Nxg2 Rg3! threatening 3 ... Rh3 mate and if 3 Nf4 Rg1 is mate.

Draughts

Puzzle 1) White wins with 1 f4-g5 f6xh4 2 h2-g3 h4xf2 3 g1xe3xc5xe7.

Puzzle 2) White wins with 1 f4-e5 d6xf4 2 e3xg5 h6xf4 3 c1xe3xg5.

IQ Tests

1. Whale. The whale is the only mammal.

2. 90, 93. The numbers alternately increase by 3 or double.

3. Hermes. All the others are planets in the solar system.

4. Optics. Acoustics is the science of sound, optics of light.

5. 39. Each subsequent number is obtained by doubling the previous one and then subtracting a number which increments by one each time (e.g. 3x2 - 1 = 5; 5x2 - 2 = 8; 8x2 - 3 = 13 etc.)

6. Aristotle. All the others are composers.

7. Rio de Janeiro. Rio is in the southern hemisphere. All the others are in the northern hemisphere.

8. 197. All the other numbers are perfect squares.

9. J. If the letters are replaced by their position in the alphabet, we get the sequence 2, 5, 10, 17, 26. Each of these is a square number plus one.

10. 22. The upper row numbers increment by 2, 3 and 4. The lower row by 3, 5 and 7.

Now check your score against the following chart:

Correct answers	1	2	3	4	5	6	7	8	9	10
IQ Rating	82	90	98	106	115	124	133	142	151	160+

Scoring 100 is average, while 130 is in the genius range (see chapter 1).

Sudoku

8	6	5	4	1	2	3	9	7
1	2	9	7	5	3	8	4	6
7	3	4	6	8	9	1	5	2
5	4	3	2	7	8	9	6	1
2	8	6	3	9	1	5	7	4
9	1	7	5	6	4	2	8	3
6	5	1	9	2	7	4	3	8
3	7	2	8	4	5	6	1	9
4	9	8	1	3	6	7	2	5

For information on all Buzan products and courses please contact us at:
email: info@buzan.org; Website: www.buzan.org

UK
Buzan Limited
54 Parkstone Road
Poole
Dorset BH15 2PG
UK
Tel: +44 (0)1202 674676
Fax: +44 (0)1202 674776

USA
Buzan Centre USA Inc
PO Box 4
Palm Beach, Florida 33480
Free Toll in USA 806-896-1024
Tel: USA 1 734 207 5287